A-Z SOUTHPORT

CW00408769

CONTENTS

Key to Map Pages	2-3
Map Pages	4-27
Ind...	
Vill...	
sel...	

REFERENCE

Motorway	M58	Car Park (selected)	P
A Road	A570	Church or Chapel	†
B Road	B5208	Fire Station	■
Dual Carriageway		Hospital	H
		Information Centre	i
One-way Street		National Grid Reference	350
Traffic flow on A Roads is indicated by a heavy line on the driver's left.	→	Park & Ride	The Esplanade P+
Restricted Access		Police Station	▲
Pedestrianized Road		Post Office	★
Track / Footpath		Toilet:	
		without facilities for the Disabled	▽
Railway	Station / Tunnel / Level Crossing	with facilities for the Disabled	▽
		Viewpoint	米 米
Built-up Area	REGENT CL.	Educational Establishment	◰
		Hospital or Hospice	◰
Local Authority Boundary	— · — · —	Industrial Building	◰
		Leisure or Recreational Facility	◰
Posttown Boundary		Place of Interest	◰
Postcode Boundary within Posttown		Public Building	◰
		Shopping Centre or Market	◰
Map Continuation	16	Other Selected Buildings	◰

SCALE

1:15,840   4 inches to 1 mile   6.31 cm to 1 km   10.16 cm to 1 mile

0   ¼   ½   ¾   1 Mile

0   250   500   750   1 Kilometre

Copyright of Geographers' A-Z Map Company Limited

Fairfield Road, Borough Green, Sevenoaks, Kent TN15 8PP
Telephone: 01732 781000 (Enquiries & Trade Sales)
01732 783422 (Retail Sales)

www.a-zmaps.co.uk

Copyright © Geographers' A-Z Map Co. Ltd.

OS Ordnance Survey   This product includes mapping data licensed from Ordnance Survey® with the permission of the Controller of Her Majesty's Stationery Office.

© Crown Copyright 2004. All rights reserved. Licence number 100017302

Edition 3 2006

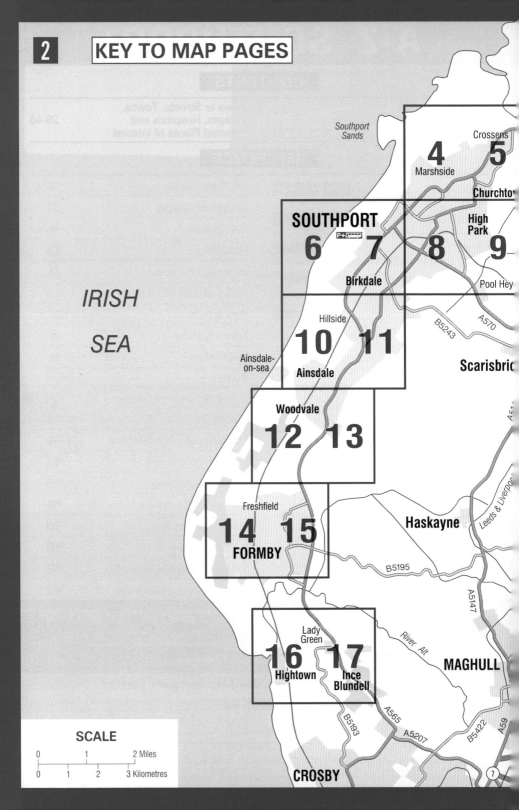

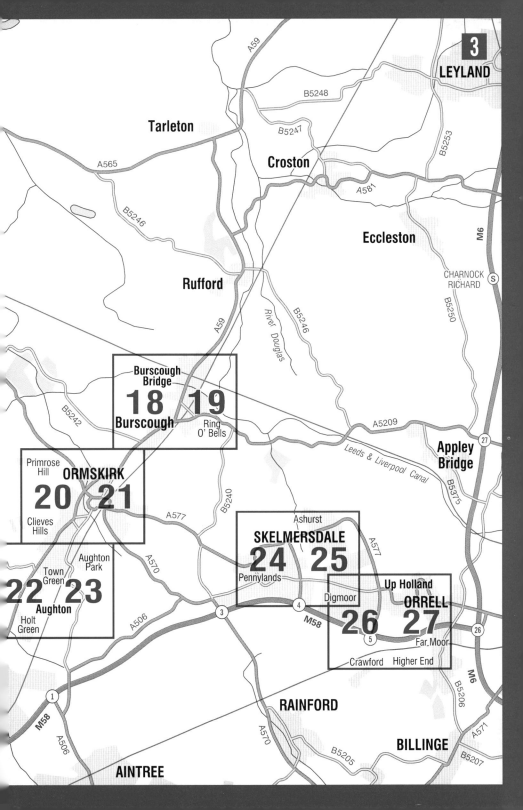

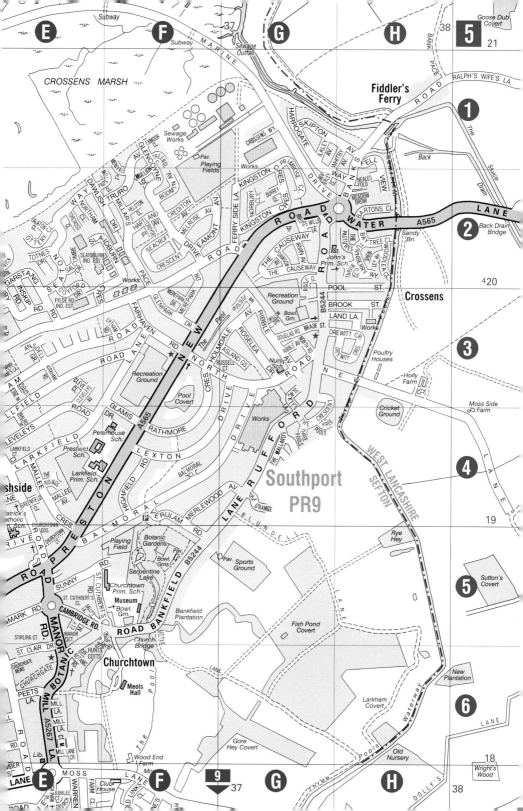

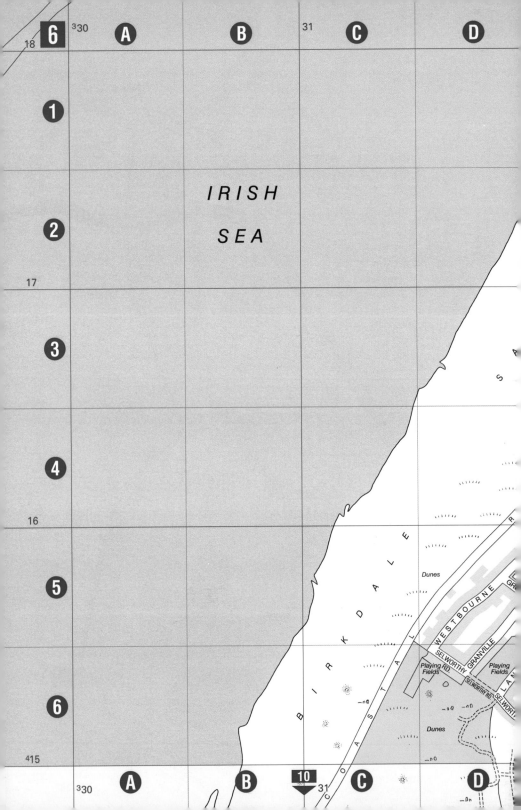

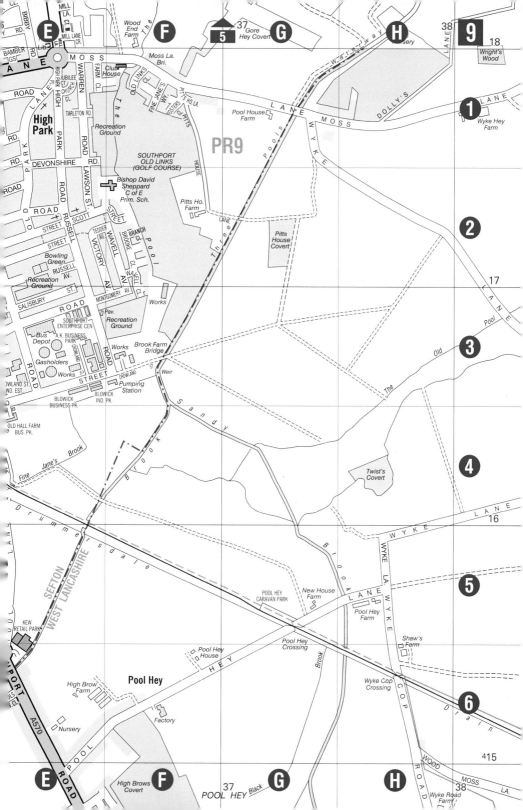

A **B** 6 31 **C** Dunes **D**

1 IRISH SEA

HILLS

ROYAL BIRKDALE GOLF COURSE

Club House

2 14

B I R K D A L E

HILLSIDE GOLF COURSE

3

BIRKDALE HILL NATURE RESERVE

4 SOUTHPORT AND GOLF COUR

13 Hawes House

Boating Lake Playing Field

SHORE Toad Hall RD. UPTON AV. Ainsdale High Sch.

The Lido PROMENADE Railway Cottages KNOWLE AVENUE Club House Recr Tennis Gr Cts.

5 COASTAL RD. ORCHATSWORTH CHILTERN RD. PETWORTH RD. CHARTWELL DR. TAVISTOCK RD. TUDOR GLENEHEM RD. SCAFIELD RD. HATFIELD CARLTON RD. OSBORNE ROAD BERWICK BRADSHAW'S LA.

STRATFORD BARFORD DANE GREENWAYS FENWAY BELVEDERE RD. FAULKNER RD. BURNLEY RD. FAIRFIELD AV. MILL HOUSE LODGE

ARDEN CL. ARLINGTON LETON DR. HARRINGTON DR. BROADWAY SANDRINGHAM ROAD Mountwood Lodge BURNLEY ROAD FAULKNERS RD. LEAMINGTON AV. JOHNS RD. LIVERPOOL AV. War Meml.

PONTINS SOUTHPORT CENTRE GRAFTON DARESBURY DR. PRESTBURY AV. KENILWORTH ROAD Sherwood RD. SANVINO AV. LIVERPOOL RD. Lib. GREEN AV. UNIT RD.

6 Ainsdale-on-Sea CHIPPING AV. CHANDLEY CL. BARRINGTON RD. DELAMERE RD. Ainsdale P Queen Charlotte Village SALFORD THE WOODLANDS LEAMINGTON AV. LIMONT

LEACH DR. ALDCROFT ARLINGTON CL. KETTERING RD. SEVENOAKS AV. MANDEVILLE RD. STATION HALIFAX RD. GREENLOONS RD. SANDBROOK

12 ROTHWELL DR. SAMBOURN CL. MERIDEN CL. WILMCOTE CL. MOSSGIEL CHESTERFIELD RD. HILLSVIEW SALFORD ROAD STOURTON ST. JOHNS CT. Sch

WESTMINSTER 12 31 BLUNDELL DONS CFT.

Ainsdale

12 29

12

AINSDALE SANDS

A I N S D A L E   H I L L S

WEST END PLANTATION

West End Lodge
Tennis Court
Windy Gap

AINSDALE SAND DUNES
NATIONAL NATURE RESERVE

Long Slack

Fire Tower

Cloven-le-Dale

Golf Cottage

FISHERMAN'S PATH

FORMBY
GOLF COURSE

WOODLAND

WOODVALE
AIRFIELD

Liverpool
L37

W h a m   Dyke

Woodvale
Aero Club

Riding School

LITTLE BREWERY

WEST
BREWERY

Playing

SIXTEEN ACRE LANE   EIGHT ACRE

EIGHT ACRE LA.

ARLINGTON CL

WESTMINSTER DR

BRINKLOW

SAMBOURN FOLD

ROTHWELL DR

RUTHWELL DR

LIGHTHORNE DR

CARLTON

PERSHORE GRO.

FRINTON

KINGSBURY CL.

SHELTON DR.

HARBURY DR.

HARBURY

HARBURY

KETTERING

KENNFORD

KENILWORTH DR

DELAMERE

10

Ainsdale

Shoreside Primary Sch.

Merefield School

Little Ball's Hill

Big Ball's Hill

MERIDEN GR.

BOSWORTH DR

WESTON AV.

EASDALE DR.

SUNBUR

MIDHURST

MARDALE CL.

WATERFORD

CASEDALE DR.

THURSBY CL.

WOODSIDE AV.

FURNESS CL.

WHITEHAVEN CL.

NEWBY CL

KENDAL

THIRLMERE

PINFOLD

Woodvale

Segar's Farm

PINFOLD LA.

CORNI

Caravan Site

SOUTHPORT

SOUTHPORT OLD ROAD

A565
F O R M B Y

Warrer House

Rose Farm

Fro Dune ath

14

15

A   B   C   D

29   330

11

410

09

1   2   3   4   5   6

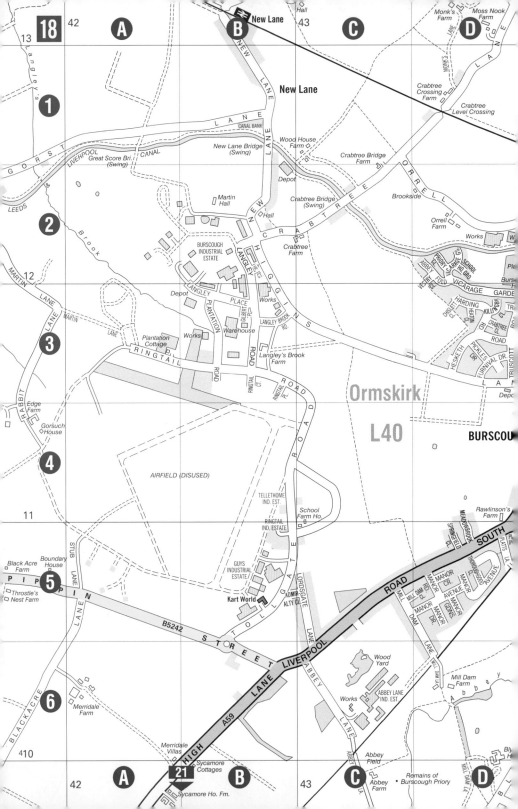

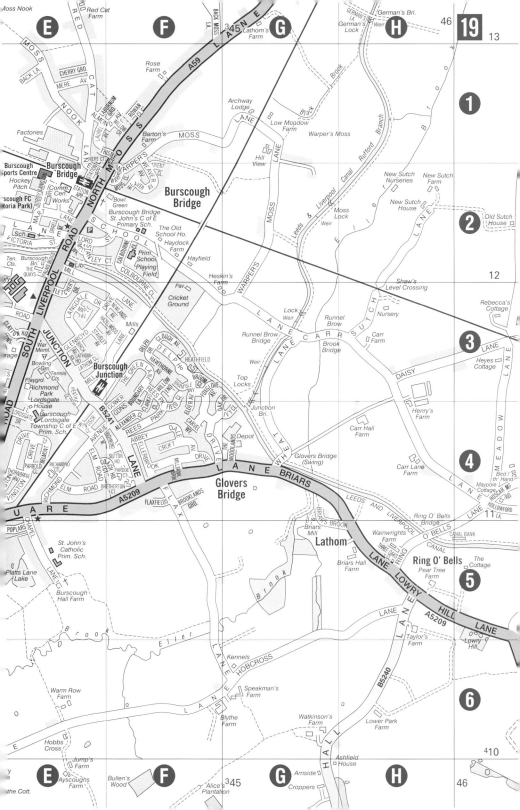

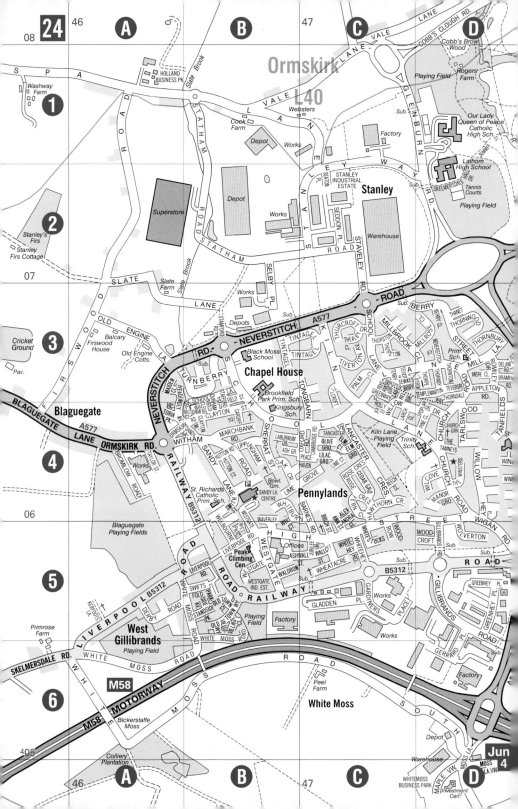

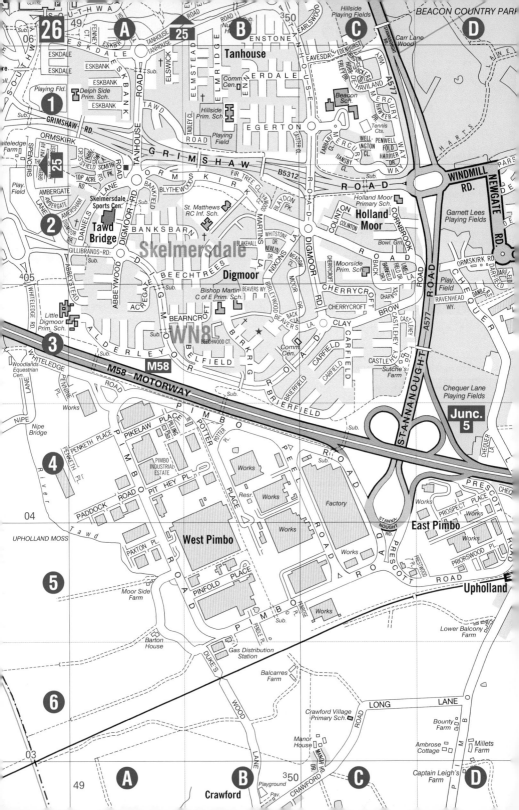

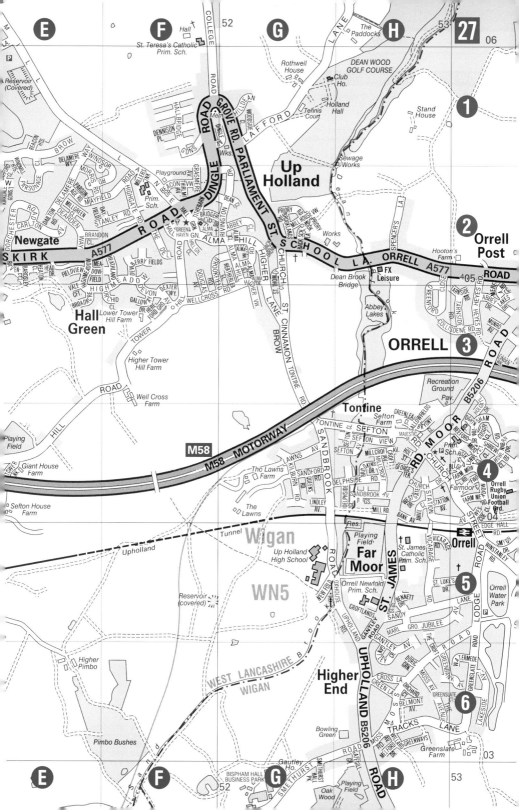

INDEX

Including Streets, Places & Areas, Hospitals & Hospices, Industrial Estates,
Selected Flats & Walkways, Stations, and Selected Places of Interest.

HOW TO USE THIS INDEX

1. Each street name is followed by its Postcode District and then by its Locality abbreviation(s) and then by its map reference;
   e.g. **Abbey Dale** L40: Burs . . . .4F **19** is in the L40 Postcode District and the Burscough Locality and is to be found in square 4F on page **19**.
   The page number is shown in bold type.

2. A strict alphabetical order is followed in which Av., Rd., St., etc. (though abbreviated) are read in full and as part of the street name;
   e.g. **Abbotsford** appears after **Abbots Cl.** but before **Abbots Way**

3. Streets and a selection of flats and walkways too small to be shown on the maps, appear in the index with the thoroughfare to which it is connected
   shown in brackets; e.g. **Alexandra B'way.** *PR9: South* . . . .*1B 8* (off Alexandra Rd.)

4. Addresses that are in more than one part are referred to as not continuous.

5. Places and areas are shown in the index in BLUE TYPE and the map reference is to the actual map square in which the town centre or area is
   located and not to the place name shown on the map; e.g. AINSDALE 6C 10

6. An example of a selected place of interest is Botanic Gardens Mus. 5F 5

7. An example of a station is **Ainsdale Station (Rail)** . . . .6C 10 Included are Rail (**Rail**) and Park & Ride (**Park & Ride**)

8. An example of a hospital is ORMSKIRK AND DISTRICT GENERAL HOSPITAL 5G 21

GENERAL ABBREVIATIONS

All. : Alley	**Est.** : Estate	**Nth.** : North
App. : Approach	**Fld.** : Field	**Pde.** : Parade
Arc. : Arcade	**Flds.** : Fields	**Pk.** : Park
Av. : Avenue	**Gdns.** : Gardens	**Pas.** : Passage
Bk. : Back	**Ga.** : Gate	**Pl.** : Place
Bri. : Bridge	**Grn.** : Green	**Rd.** : Road
B'way. : Broadway	**Gro.** : Grove	**Shop.** : Shopping
Bldgs. : Buildings	**Hgts.** : Heights	**Sth.** : South
Bus. : Business	**Ho.** : House	**Sq.** : Square
Cvn. : Caravan	**Ind.** : Industrial	**St.** : Street
C'way. : Causeway	**Info.** : Information	**Ter.** : Terrace
Cen. : Centre	**La.** : Lane	**Trad.** : Trading
Chu. : Church	**Lit.** : Little	**Up.** : Upper
Cl. : Close	**Lwr.** : Lower	**Vw.** : View
Comn. : Common	**Mnr.** : Manor	**Vs.** : Villas
Cotts. : Cottages	**Mans.** : Mansions	**Wlk.** : Walk
Ct. : Court	**Mdw.** : Meadow	**W.** : West
Cres. : Crescent	**M.** : Mews	**Yd.** : Yard
Cft. : Croft	**Mt.** : Mount	
Dr. : Drive	**Mus.** : Museum	

LOCALITY ABBREVIATIONS

Ains : **Ainsdale**	Dalt : **Dalton**	Orm : **Ormskirk**
Augh : **Aughton**	Form : **Formby**	Orr : **Orrell**
Banks : **Banks**	Gt Alt : **Great Altcar**	Scar : **Scarisbrick**
Bart : **Barton**	Hals : **Halsall**	Skel : **Skelmersdale**
Bic : **Bickerstaffe**	High : **Hightown**	South : **Southport**
Bil : **Billinge**	Ince B : **Ince Blundell**	Thorn : **Thornton**
B'dale : **Birkdale**	Lath : **Lathom**	Uph : **Upholland**
Burs : **Burscough**	Lit C : **Little Crosby**	Westh : **Westhead**
Chu : **Churchtown**	Lyd : **Lydiate**	
Cros : **Crossens**	Marsh : **Marshside**	

A

Abbey Cl. L37: Form 5G 15	
WN8: Uph 2G 27	
Abbey Dale L40: Burs 4F 19	
Abbey Dr. WN5: Orr 3H 27	
Abbey Fold L40: Burs 2D 18	
Abbey Gdns. PR8: B'dale 5G 7	
Abbey La. L40: Burs, Lath 6C 18	
Abbey La. Ind. Est. L40: Burs 6C 18	
Abbeystead WN8: Skel 6F 25	
Abbeywood WN8: Skel 3A 26	
Abbots Cl. L37: Form 6F 15	
Abbotsford L39: Orm 4F 21	
Abbots Way L37: Form 6F 15	
Academy, The PR9: South 1A 8	
Acorns, The L39: Augh 6C 20	
Acregate WN8: Skel 3A 26	
Acre Gro. PR8: B'dale 6F 7	

Admiralty Cl. L40: Burs 5B 18	
Aindow Ct. PR8: B'dale 6F 7	
AINSDALE 6C 10	
AINSDALE-ON-SEA 6A 10	
Ainsdale Sand Dunes National Nature Reserve	
. . . . .4A 12	
Ainsdale Station (Rail) 6C 10	
Aintree Cres. PR8: South 5D 8	
AK Bus. Pk. PR9: South 3E 9	
Albany Rd. PR9: South 6A 4	
Albert Ct. PR9: South 6B 4	
Albert Pl. PR9: South 1H 7	
Albert Rd. L37: Form 6A 14	
PR9: South 1A 8	
Albert Ter. PR8: B'dale 4G 7	
Alderdale Av. PR8: Ains 6A 10	
Alder La. L39: Bart 6G 13	
Alderley WN8: Skel 3A 26	
Alderson Cres. L37: Form 3E 15	
Alexander Cl. L40: Burs 4F 19	

Alexandra B'way. PR9: South 1B 8	
(off Alexandra Rd.)	
Alexandra Cl. WN8: Skel 4C 24	
Alexandra Ct. PR9: South 1B 8	
Alexandra M. L39: Orm 3E 21	
PR9: South 1A 8	
Alexandra Rd. L37: Form 6A 14	
L40: Burs 3D 18	
PR9: South 6A 4	
Allerton Rd. PR9: South 6C 4	
Alma Cl. WN8: Uph 2G 27	
Alma Ct. PR8: Ains 4F 11	
WN8: Uph 2G 27	
Alma Grn. WN8: Uph 2F 27	
Alma Hill WN8: Uph 2F 27	
Alma Pde. WN8: Uph 2G 27	
Alma Rd. PR8: B'dale 5G 7	
WN8: Uph 2G 27	
Alma Wlk. WN8: Uph 2G 27	
Almond Av. L40: Burs 1E 19	

Alston Ct. PR8: Ains 5E 11
Altcar La. L37: Form 3H 15
   (Downholland Moss La.)
L37: Form .6E 15
   (Hoggs Hill La.)
Altcar Rifle Range Est. L38: High 2B 16
Altcar Rd. L37: Form 5F 15
Altham Rd. PR8: South 6C 8
Althorpe Dr. PR8: South 6C 8
Alton Cl. L38: High 5B 16
Alt Rd. L37: Form 5F 15
L38: High .3B 16
   (not continuous)
Altys La. L39: Orm 5F 21
Ambergate WN8: Skel 6F 25
Amersham WN8: Skel 6F 25
Anchor Ct. PR8: B'dale 4F 7
Anchor St. PR9: South 2H 7
Andreas Cl. PR8: B'dale 5H 7
Andrews Cl. L37: Form 6D 14
Andrews La. L37: Form 5D 14
Andrews Yort L37: Form 6D 14
Annandale Gdns. WN8: Uph 2D 26
Anne Av. PR8: Ains 5E 11
Annexe, The PR9: South 1A 8
   (off Hoghton Gro.)
Ann St. WN8: Skel 5C 24
Ansdell Gro. PR9: Chu 3E 5
Anvil Cl. WN5: Orr 4H 27
Apartments, The PR9: South 1H 7
Appleton Rd. WN8: Skel 3D 24
Arbour St. PR8: South 3A 8
Arden Cl. PR8: Ains 6A 10
Ardleigh Av. WN8: Skel 6C 8
Argameols Cl. PR8: South 4D 8
Argameols Gro. L37: Form 2D 14
Argameols Rd. L37: Form 1D 14
Argyle Ct. PR9: South 5B 4
Argyle Lawn Tennis Club 5C 4
Argyle Pk. PR9: South 1B 8
Argyle Rd. PR9: South 6B 4
Arlington Cl. PR8: Ains 6A 10
Arnian Ct. L39: Augh 3E 23
Arnside Rd. PR9: South 2A 8
Arnside Ter. PR9: South 2A 8
Arundel Rd. PR8: B'dale 3F 11
Ascot Cl. PR8: B'dale 4E 7
Ash Cl. L39: Orm 4D 20
Ashcroft Av. L39: Orm 3F 21
Ashcroft Rd. L37: Form 6E 15
Ashdale Cl. L37: Form 5B 14
Ashdown Cl. PR8: South 5C 8
Ash Gro. L37: Form 6B 14
WN8: Skel 4B 24
Ashley Rd. PR9: South 2A 8
WN8: Skel 2F 25
Ashmead Rd. WN8: Skel 1E 25
Ash St. PR8: South 4A 8
Ashton Pl. PR8: South 3H 7
Ashton Rd. PR8: B'dale 2F 11
Ashton's La. L37: Form 6B 14
ASHURST 1F 25
Ashurst Cl. WN8: Skel 1F 25
Ashurst Ct. L37: Form 5D 14
Ashurst Gdns. WN8: Skel 1F 25
Ashurst Rd. WN8: Skel 2F 25
Ashwall St. WN8: Skel 5B 24
Ashwood WN8: Skel 2G 25
Asland Gdns. PR9: Cros 3G 5
Asmall Cl. L39: Orm 3D 20
Asmall La. L39: Hals 1A 20
L39: Orm, Scar 1A 20
L40: Hals, Scar 1A 20
Aspen Gro. L37: Form 6B 14
Aspen Way WN8: Skel 3C 24
Athole Gro. PR9: South 2D 8
Atkinson Art Gallery 2H 7
   (within Gallery)
AUGHTON 4C 22
Aughton M. PR8: B'dale 4G 7
AUGHTON PARK 1F 23
Aughton Pk. Dr. L39: Augh 1F 23
Aughton Park Station (Rail) 1F 23
Aughton Rd. PR8: B'dale 3F 7

Aughton St. L39: Orm 5D 20
   (not continuous)
Avenue, The L39: Orm 3D 20
   (Halsall La.)
L39: Orm .3E 21
   (Southport Rd.)
WN5: Bil .6H 27
Avondale Rd. PR9: South 1H 7
Avondale Rd. Nth. PR9: South 6A 4
Ayr Cl. PR8: South 5D 8

B

Bk. Bath St. PR9: South 1H 7
Bk. Botanic Rd. PR9: Chu 5F 5
Back Brow WN8: Uph 2G 27
Bk. Compton Rd. PR8: B'dale 6H 7
Bk. Forest Rd. PR8: South 3B 8
   (not continuous)
Back La. L39: Augh 4A 22
L40: Burs 1E 19
WN8: Skel 3B 26
   (Beavers La.)
WN8: Skel 2C 26
   (School La.)
Bk. Moss La. L40: Burs 1F 19
Bk. o' the Town La. L38: Ince B 4G 17
Bk. School La. WN8: Skel 4B 24
WN8: Uph 2G 27
Bk. Virginia St. PR8: South 3A 8
Badgers Rake L37: Form 2B 14
Bakers La. PR9: Chu 4D 4
Balfour Rd. PR8: South 4C 8
Ball's Pl. PR8: South 2H 7
Balmoral Cl. PR9: Chu 4F 5
Balmoral Dr. L37: Form 6D 14
PR9: Chu 5E 5
Bamber Gdns. PR9: Chu 1E 9
Banastre Rd. PR8: South 4G 7
Bank Av. WN5: Orr 4H 27
Bankfield WN8: Skel 6G 25
Bankfield La. PR9: Chu 5F 5
Bank Nook PR9: Chu 4C 4
   (not continuous)
Bank Pace PR9: Banks 1H 5
Bank Pas. PR8: South 2H 7
Banksbarn WN8: Skel 6G 25
Bankside L38: High 4B 16
Bank Sq. PR9: South 1H 7
Banks Rd. PR9: Cros, Banks 2H 5
Bannatyne's Health Club 3F 25
Bardsley Cl. WN8: Uph 2E 27
Barford Cl. PR8: Ains 5A 10
WN8: Uph 2E 27
Barkfield Av. L37: Form 3D 14
Barkfield La. L37: Form 3C 14
Barnes Rd. L39: Augh 6E 21
WN8: Skel 4C 24
Barnfield Dr. WN8: Skel 2C 26
Barns, The L37: Form 6F 15
Barrett Av. PR8: B'dale 1G 11
Barrett Rd. PR8: B'dale 1G 11
Barrington Dr. PR8: Ains 6B 10
Barton Heys Rd. L37: Form 6C 14
Bartons Cl. PR9: Cros 2H 5
Bath Springs L39: Orm 4F 21
Bath Springs Ct. L39: Orm 4F 21
Bath St. PR9: South 1H 7
Bath St. Nth. PR9: South 1H 7
Battle Way L37: Form 5G 15
Baytree Cl. PR9: Cros 2H 5
Beacham Rd. PR8: South 2C 8
Beach M. PR8: B'dale 3F 7
Beach Priory Gdns. PR8: South 3F 7
Beach Rd. PR8: B'dale 3F 7
Beacon Country Pk. 1D 26
Beacon Hgts. WN8: Uph 1E 27
Beacon La. WN8: Skel 1G 25
Beacons, The L37: Form 4E 15
   (off School La.)
Beaconsfield Ct. L39: Orm 4F 21
Beaconsfield Rd. PR9: South 3D 8
Beacon Vw. Dr. WN8: Uph 2F 27

Bearncroft WN8: Skel 3A 26
Beatty Rd. PR8: South 4C 8
Beaufort L37: Form 5F 15
Beaufort Cl. L39: Augh 2C 22
Beaumont Cres. L39: Augh 1F 23
Beavers La. WN8: Skel 3B 26
Beavers Way WN8: Skel 3B 26
Bebles Rd. L39: Orm 6C 20
Bedford Ct. PR8: B'dale 1G 11
Bedford Rd. PR8: B'dale 1G 11
Beech Cl. WN8: Skel 4C 24
Beech Ct. PR9: South 1B 8
Beech Dr. L37: Form 3C 14
Beechfield Gdns. PR8: South 3F 7
Beechfield M. PR9: South 2H 7
Beech Gro. PR9: South 2C 8
Beech Mdw. L39: Orm 5G 21
Beech Rd. L39: Augh 5C 22
Beechtrees WN8: Skel 6G 25
Beechwood WN8: Skel 2G 25
Beechwood Ct. WN8: Skel 3B 26
Beechwood Dr. L37: Form 5C 14
L39: Orm .4D 20
Beeford Dr. WN5: Orr 4H 27
Belfield WN8: Skel 3B 26
Belgrave Pl. PR8: B'dale 6F 7
Belgrave Pl. PR8: B'dale 6F 7
Bellis Av. PR9: Chu 5D 4
Belmont Av. WN5: Bil 6H 27
Belmont Cl. L40: Burs 4E 19
Belmont St. PR8: South 3G 7
Belvedere Dr. L37: Form 6E 15
Belvedere Pk. L39: Augh 4E 23
Belvedere Rd. PR8: Ains 6C 10
Bengarth Rd. PR9: South 1D 8
Bennett Dr. WN5: Orr 5H 27
Bentham St. PR8: South 4H 7
Bentham's Way PR8: South 1H 11
Beresford Dr. PR9: Chu 6D 4
Beresford Gdns. PR9: Chu 5D 4
Berry Cl. WN8: Skel 3D 24
Berry St. WN8: Skel 3D 24
Berwick Av. PR8: Ains 5D 10
Berwyn Ct. PR8: South 5B 8
Betty Ann Ct. PR9: South 1H 7
Beverley Cl. PR9: Cros 2G 5
Bewcastle Dr. L40: Westh 6H 21
Bibby Rd. PR9: Chu 5E 5
Bickerton Rd. PR8: B'dale 5F 7
Billinge La. L39: Bic 6G 23
Bill's La. L37: Form 6E 15
Birch Av. L40: Burs 3E 19
Birches, The L37: Form 2D 14
BIRCH GREEN .3G 25
Birch Grn. L37: Form 2C 14
Birch Grn. Rd. WN8: Skel 2F 25
Birch St. PR8: South 5H 7
WN8: Skel 4C 24
Bird i' th' Hand Cotts. L39: Orm 3E 21
BIRKDALE 5G 7
Birkdale Hill Nature Reserve 4A 10
Birkdale Station (Rail) 5G 7
Birkdale Trad. Est. PR8: B'dale 1G 11
Birkey La. L37: Form 5E 15
Birkrig WN8: Skel 3B 26
Birley Ct. PR8: South 4H 7
Birleywood WN8: Skel 3B 26
Bispham Hall Bus. Pk. WN5: Bil 6G 27
Bispham Rd. PR9: South 2D 8
Blackacre La. L39: Orm 1E 21
L40: Burs 6A 18
Blackledge Cl. WN5: Orr 4H 27
Black Moss La. L39: Augh, Orm 6D 20
BLAGUEGATE .4A 24
Blaguegate La. WN8: Skel 4A 24
Blairgowrie Gdns. L39: Orm 5G 21
Blair Gro. PR9: South 2D 8
Blakehall WN8: Skel 6H 25
Blandford Cl. PR8: B'dale 4F 7
Blaydon Pk. WN8: Skel 6H 25
Bleasdale Cl. L39: Augh 4F 23
Blenheim Rd. PR8: Ains 5B 10
Blindman's La. L39: Orm 2C 20
BLOWICK 3C 8

Blowick Bus. Pk. PR9: South 3E 9
Blowick Ind. Pk. PR9: South 3E 9
Blundell Av. L37: Form 3A 14
  L38: High 4B 16
  PR8: B'dale .1F 11
Blundell Cres. PR8: B'dale 1F 11
Blundell Dr. PR8: B'dale 1F 11
Blundell Gro. L38: High 4B 16
Blundell La. PR9: Chu 4G 5
Blundell Links Ct. PR8: Ains 1E 13
Blundell Rd. L38: High 4B 16
Blundellsands Sailing Club 5B 16
Blythe La. L40: Lath 6D 18
Blythe M. PR8: B'dale 3G 11
Blythewood WN8: Skel 6G 25
Bobby Langton Way L40: Burs 2E 19
Bodmin Av. PR9: Marsh 2F 5
Bold La. L39: Augh 4C 22
Bold St. PR9: South 1H 7
Bolton Cl. L37: Form 5F 15
Bolton Rd. PR8: B'dale 5G 7
Booth's La. L39: Augh 4A 20
Booth St. PR9: South 1H 7
Borrowdale L37: Form 2E 15
Bosworth Dr. PR8: Ains 1D 12
Botanic Gardens 5F 5
Botanic Gardens Mus. 5F 5
Botanic Rd. PR9: Chu 6E 5
Boundary La. L40: Burs 3F 19
Boundary St. PR8: South 5H 7
BOWKER'S GREEN 6F 23
Bowker's Grn. La. L39: Augh, Bic 6F 23
Bowland Ct. *PR9: South* *1A 8*
                  (off Gordon St.)
Bowling Grn. Cl. PR8: South 4D 8
Bowness Av. PR8: Ains 2E 13
Bracebridge Dr. PR8: South 6D 8
Brackenway L37: Form 1F 15
Bracknel Way L39: Augh 2C 22
Brade St. PR9: Cros 3G 5
Bradley Pl. *PR8: South* *2H 7*
               (off Eastbank St.)
Bradley St. PR9: South 1A 8
Bradshaw's La. PR8: Ains 5D 10
Braemar Av. PR9: Chu 5D 4
             (not continuous)
Bramble Way L40: Burs 3F 19
Bramhall Rd. WN8: Skel 3D 24
Brandon Cl. WN8: Uph 2E 27
Bredon Ct. L37: Form 3D 14
Breeze Rd. PR8: B'dale 1E 11
Brentwood Cl. L38: High 5B 16
Brentwood Ct. PR9: South 1B 8
Bretherton Ct. L40: Burs 4F 19
Bretton Fold PR8: South 4D 8
Brewery La. L37: Form 1E 15
Briar Rd. PR8: Ains 1F 13
Briars, The PR8: B'dale 2F 11
Briars Brook L40: Lath 4G 19
Briars Grn. WN8: Skel 1F 25
Briars La. L40: Lath 4G 19
Briary Cft. L38: High 4B 16
Brickmakers Arms Yd. *L39: Orm* *3D 20*
              (off Asmall La.)
Bridge Av. L39: Orm 4E 21
Bridge Gro. PR8: South 3H 7
Bridgehall Dr. WN8: Uph 2F 27
Bridge Ho. L39: Orm 5E 21
Bridgend Dr. PR8: Ains 1D 12
Bridge St. L39: Orm 5E 21
  PR8: South 3H 7
Bridgewills La. PR9: Cros 2G 5
Brierfield WN8: Skel 3B 26
Brighouse Cl. L39: Orm 4D 20
Brighton Rd. PR8: B'dale 6G 7
Bright St. PR9: South 2D 8
Brinklow Cl. PR8: Ains 6A 10
British Lawnmower Mus. 4H 7
Broadacre WN8: Uph 3E 27
Broadlands PR8: B'dale 6E 7
Broad La. L37: Form 6D 12
  L39: Bart 6D 12
Broadway Cl. PR8: Ains 6B 10
Brocklebank Rd. PR9: South 6C 4

Bromilow Rd. WN8: Skel 4A 24
Brompton Rd. PR8: South 2C 8
Brookdale PR8: Ains 2F 13
Brooke Cl. PR9: South 2F 9
Brook Farm Cl. L39: Orm 5E 21
Brookfield Rd. WN8: Uph 2F 27
Brook Ho. PR8: South 4A 8
Brookhouse Rd. L39: Orm 3D 20
Brooklands L39: Orm 3G 21
Brooklands Dr. WN5: Orr 4H 27
Brooklands Gro. L40: Lath 4F 19
Brooklands Rd. WN8: Uph 2G 27
Brook La. L39: Orm 5E 21
Brookside Rd. PR8: South 2H 11
Brooks Rd. L37: Form 5C 14
Brook St. PR9: Cros 3H 5
Brooks Way L37: Form 5C 14
Broom Cl. L40: Burs 3F 19
Broome Cl. PR8: B'dale 6H 7
Broome Rd. PR8: B'dale 6H 7
Broughton Av. PR8: South 5B 8
Brows Cl. L37: Form 5D 14
Brows La. L37: Form 5D 14
Bryony Cl. WN5: Orr 4H 27
Buckfast Dr. L37: Form 5G 15
Buckingham Gro. L37: Form 6D 14
Bull Cop L37: Form 4F 15
Burlington Av. L37: Form 4G 15
Burlington Rd. PR8: B'dale 6F 7
Burnley Av. PR8: Ains 6D 10
Burnley Rd. PR8: Ains 6C 10
BURSCOUGH 3E 19
BURSCOUGH BRIDGE 2D 18
Burscough Bridge Station (Rail) 2E 19
Burscough FC 2E 19
Burscough Ind. Est. L40: Burs 2B 18
Burscough Junction Station (Rail) 3E 19
Burscough Rd. L39: Orm 3F 21
Burscough Sports Cen. 2E 19
Burscough St. L39: Orm 4E 21
Burwell Av. L37: Form 6C 14
Bury Rd. PR8: B'dale 6H 7
Bushbys La. L37: Form 5B 14
Bushbys Pk. L37: Form 5B 14
Butcher's La. L39: Augh 6B 22
Butterfield Gdns. L39: Augh 6D 20
Buttermere Cl. L37: Form 4C 14
Butts La. PR8: South 4D 8
Byland Cl. L37: Form 5G 15
Byrom St. PR9: South 2D 8
Byron Cl. L37: Form 3E 15

C

Cable M. *PR8: South* *2H 7*
              (off Cable St.)
Cable St. L37: Form 3F 15
  PR9: South 2H 7
Caister Cl. WN8: Skel 5H 25
Calder Av. L39: Orm 6D 20
Camberley Cl. PR8: B'dale 4E 7
Cambrian Ct. PR9: South 1B 8
Cambridge Arc. PR8: South 2H 7
Cambridge Av. PR9: Chu 5D 4
Cambridge Ct. PR9: Chu 5D 4
Cambridge Gdns. PR9: Chu 5D 4
Cambridge Rd. L37: Form 6B 14
  PR9: Chu, South 6C 4
  WN8: Skel 4C 24
Cambridge Walks *PR8: South* *2H 7*
            (off Cambridge Arc.)
Canal Bank L40: Burs 1B 18
  L40: Lath 5H 19
Canning Rd. PR9: South 2E 9
Canterbury Rd. L37: Form 1E 15
  PR8: B'dale 5F 7
Cantlow Fold PR8: Ains 1C 12
Capilano Pk. L39: Augh 3E 23
Cardiff St. WN8: Skel 4B 24
Cardigan Rd. PR8: B'dale 2F 11
Carfield WN8: Skel 3C 26
Carisbrooke Dr. PR9: Chu 6D 4

Carlisle Rd. PR8: B'dale 1G 11
Carlton Av. WN8: Uph 2E 27
Carlton Rd. PR8: Ains 5C 10
Carmel Cl. L39: Augh 1F 23
Carnarvon Rd. PR8: B'dale 2F 11
Carneghie Ct. PR8: B'dale 5F 7
Carnoustie Cl. PR8: B'dale 5F 7
Carr Ho. La. L38: Ince B 3G 17
CARR HOUSES .3H 17
Carr La. L40: Lath 3G 19
  PR8: Ains 4F 11
           (not continuous)
Carr Moss La. L39: Hals 1H 13
Carroll Cres. L39: Orm 2F 21
Carr's Cres. L37: Form 6D 14
Carr's Cres. W. L37: Form 6C 14
Carr Side La. L29: Thorn 4H 17
Carrwood Pk. PR8: South 6H 7
Cartmel Cl. PR8: South 6D 8
Cartmel Dr. L37: Form 5G 15
Carvel Way L40: Burs 4F 19
Castle Dr. L37: Form 6E 15
Castlehey WN8: Skel 3C 26
Castle St. PR9: South 1H 7
Castle Wlk. PR8: South 3G 7
Catharine's La. L39: Bic 1H 23
Caton Cl. PR9: Marsh 3D 4
Cattan Grn. L37: Form 4G 15
Catterick Fold PR8: South 6D 8
Causeway, The PR9: Cros 2G 5
Cavendish Ct. PR9: South 6C 4
Cavendish Rd. PR8: B'dale 5F 7
Cedar Cres. L39: Orm 5D 20
Cedar Dr. L37: Form 6B 14
Cedar Gro. WN8: Skel 4C 24
Cedar St. PR8: South 5A 8
Cemetery Rd. PR8: South 5H 7
Central 12 Retail Pk. PR9: South 2A 8
Central Av. PR8: B'dale 3F 11
Chambres Rd. PR8: South 4B 8
Chambres Rd. Nth. PR8: South 3B 8
Chandley Cl. PR8: Ains 6A 10
Chapel Ct. L39: Orm 5F 21
Chapel Gallery, The 4F 21
CHAPEL HOUSE .4B 24
Chapelhouse Wlk. L37: Form 4F 15
Chapel La. L37: Form 4E 15
  L40: Burs 5E 19
Chapel M. L39: Orm 5F 21
Chapel Moss L39: Orm 5E 21
Chapel St. L39: Orm 5F 21
  PR8: South 2H 7
Charles Av. PR8: South 5E 11
Charlesbye Av. L39: Orm 3G 21
Charlesbye Cl. L39: Orm 3H 21
Charles Ct. PR9: South 2A 8
Charnock WN8: Skel 3C 26
Chartwell Rd. PR8: Ains 5B 10
Chase Cl. PR8: B'dale 5F 7
Chase Heys PR9: Chu 6D 4
Chatsworth Rd. PR8: Ains 5A 10
Cheapside L37: Form 5F 15
Cheltenham Way PR8: South 5D 8
Chequer Cl. WN8: Uph 4D 26
Chequer La. WN8: Uph 2D 26
Cheriton Pk. PR8: South 6C 8
Cherrycroft WN8: Skel 3C 26
Cherry Grn. L39: Augh 2D 22
Cherry Gro. L40: Burs 1E 19
Cherry Rd. PR8: Ains 3F 13
Cherry Tree La. L39: Augh 2D 22
Chester Av. PR9: South 1C 8
Chesterfield Cl. PR8: Ains 1D 12
Chesterfield Rd. PR8: Ains 1D 12
Chester Rd. PR9: South 1D 8
Chestnut Ct. L39: Orm 3F 21
  PR9: South 1A 8
Chestnut Grange L39: Orm 6D 20
Chestnut St. PR8: South 4A 8
Chestnut Way L37: Form 6B 14
Chiltern Rd. PR8: Ains 5A 10
Chindit Cl. L37: Form 5C 14
Chipping Av. PR8: Ains 6A 10
Chislett Cl. L40: Burs 3D 18

Christines Cres. L40: Burs 3D 18
Chromolyte Ind. Est. PR8: South 4H 7
Church Cl. L37: Form 4F 15
  PR9: South .1E 9
Church Cl. Ct. L37: Form 4F 15
Church Dr. WN5: Orr 4H 27
Church Flds. L39: Orm 4E 21
Churchfields PR8: B'dale 6F 7
Churchgate PR9: Chu 6D 4
  (not continuous)
Churchgate M. PR9: Chu 6E 5
Church Grn. L37: Form 5B 14
  WN8: Skel .4D 24
Church Hill Rd. L39: Orm 3D 20
Churchill Av. PR9: Chu 5D 4
Church La. L39: Augh 4C 22
Church Path L37: Form 2E 15
Church Rd. L37: Form 3F 15
  WN8: Skel .4D 24
Church St. L39: Orm 4E 21
  PR9: South .2A 8
  WN5: Orr 4H 27
  WN8: Uph 2G 27
CHURCHTOWN 6E 5
Churchtown Ct. PR9: Chu 5E 5
Churchtown Gdns. PR9: Chu 4E 5
Church Vw. L39: Augh 4C 22
Church Vw. Ct. L39: Orm 4E 21
  (off Burscough St.)
Church Walks L39: Orm 4E 21
Church Way L37: Form 5B 14
Cinnamon Brow WN8: Uph 3G 27
Cirrus Dr. L39: Augh 2C 22
Clairville PR8: B'dale 4F 7
Claremont Av. PR8: B'dale 5G 7
Claremont Dr. L39: Augh 6D 20
Claremont Gdns. PR8: B'dale 5G 7
Claremont Rd. PR8: B'dale 5G 7
Clarence Rd. PR8: B'dale 5G 7
Clarkfield Cl. L40: Burs 4F 19
Clay Brow Rd. WN8: Skel 3C 26
Clayton Ho. Gdns. L40: Burs 3E 19
Clayton M. WN8: Skel 4B 24
Clayton St. WN8: Skel 4B 24
Clegg St. WN8: Skel 4B 24
Clenger's Brow PR9: Chu 5D 4
Cleveleys Av. PR9: Chu 3E 5
Cleveleys Rd. PR9: Chu 4E 5
Cleve Way L37: Form 5G 15
CLIEVES HILLS 6A 20
Clieves Hills La. L39: Augh 1A 22
Clifden Ct. L37: Form 4E 15
Clifford Rd. PR8: B'dale 2G 11
Cliff Rd. PR9: South 5B 4
Clifton Rd. L37: Form 2F 15
  PR8: South .3D 8
Clinning Rd. PR8: B'dale 1G 11
Clive Lodge PR8: B'dale 1F 11
Clive Rd. PR8: B'dale 1F 11
Cloister Grn. L37: Form 5G 15
Cloisters, The L37: Form 4E 15
  PR9: South .1A 8
  (off Hoghton Gro.)
Close, The L38: Ince B 4G 17
Clough Av. L40: Burs 3F 19
Clovelly Dr. PR8: B'dale 3E 11
Clucas Gdns. L39: Orm 3E 21
Coach Ho. Ct. L40: Burs 4F 19
Coastal Rd. PR8: Ains, B'dale 5A 10
Coastline M. PR9: Chu 3E 5
Cobbs Clough Rd. L40: Lath 1D 24
Cobden Rd. PR9: South 3D 8
Cockle Dick's La. PR9: Chu 5C 4
Colbourne Cl. L40: Burs 4F 19
Colchester Rd. PR8: South 6D 8
Cole Cres. L39: Augh 3E 23
Colinmander Gdns. L39: Orm 6C 20
Colinton WN8: Skel 2C 26
College Av. L37: Form 2D 14
College Cl. L37: Form 3C 14
  PR8: B'dale .6G 7
College Path L37: Form 2C 14
College Rd. WN8: Uph 1F 27
Collisdene Rd. WN5: Orr 3H 27

Compton Rd. PR8: B'dale 6H 7
Concourse Shop. Cen., The
  WN8: Skel .4F 25
Conifer Ct. L37: Form 5E 15
Coniston Ct. PR8: Ains 2E 13
Coniston Rd. L37: Form 5C 14
Convent Cl. L39: Augh 1G 23
Conyers Av. PR8: B'dale 6F 7
Coppice Leys L37: Form 4D 14
Cornbrook WN8: Skel 2C 26
Cornwall Way PR8: Ains 2D 12
Coronation Av. L37: Form 5F 15
Coronation Wlk. PR8: South 2G 7
Corporation St. PR8: South 2H 7
Cosgate Cl. WN5: Orr 4H 27
Cottage Cl. L39: Orm 5D 20
Cottage La. L39: Orm 3D 20
Cottage M. L39: Orm 4D 20
Cotton Dr. L39: Orm 3D 20
Cottys Brow PR9: Chu 4D 4
Coudray Rd. PR9: South 6C 4
County Rd. L39: Orm 5D 20
Courtfield L39: Orm 2D 20
Court Grn. L39: Orm 2D 20
Court M. PR9: Chu 6E 5
Court Rd. PR9: South 1A 8
Courtyard, The PR9: South 2H 7
Coyford Dr. PR9: Marsh 3E 5
Crabtree Cl. L40: Burs 3D 18
Crabtree La. L40: Burs 2B 18
CRAWFORD 6B 26
Crawford Rd. WN8: Skel 6B 26
Crediton Av. PR9: Marsh 2F 5
Crescent, The PR9: Cros 4G 5
Crescent Av. L37: Form 6D 14
Crescent Grn. L39: Augh 2D 22
Crescent Rd. PR8: B'dale 6F 7
Cricket Path L37: Form 2E 15
  PR8: B'dale .6F 7
Crockleford Av. PR8: South 6C 8
Croft, The WN5: Bil 5H 27
Croft Av. L40: Burs 4F 19
  WN5: Orr 4H 27
Croft Heys L39: Augh 2D 22
Croftlands WN5: Orr 5H 27
Croftson Av. L39: Orm 3F 21
Cromer Rd. PR8: B'dale 1E 11
Cromfield L39: Augh 1E 23
Cromwell Cl. L39: Augh 1E 23
Croppers La. L39: Bic 2H 23
Cropton Rd. L37: Form 4E 15
Crosby Coastal Pk. 6B 16
Crosby Rd. PR8: B'dale 6F 7
Cross, The L38: Ince B 4F 17
Cross Barn La. L38: Ince B 5G 17
CROSSENS 3G 5
Crossens Way PR9: Cros 1G 5
Crossfield WN8: Skel 5G 25
Cross Grn. L37: Form 5F 15
Cross Grn. Cl. L37: Form 5F 15
Crosshall Brow L39: Orm 5H 21
  L40: Westh .5H 21
Cross La. WN5: Bil 6H 27
Cross St. PR8: South 3H 7
Croston's Brow PR9: Chu 4D 4
Crowland Cl. PR9: South 3E 9
Crowland St. PR9: South 4D 8
Crowland St. Ind. Est. PR9: South 3E 9
Crowland Way L37: Form 5G 15
Crown Cl. L37: Form 5F 15
Croxton Ct. PR9: South 6C 4
Croyde Cl. PR9: Marsh 2F 5
Cumberland Rd. PR8: South 4B 8
Cummins Av. L37: Form 2D 14
Curzon Rd. PR8: South 4B 8
Cut La. L39: Hals 1A 20
Cygnet Cl. L39: Augh 1E 23
Cypress Rd. PR8: South 3C 8

D

Dailton Rd. WN8: Uph 2E 27
Daisy La. L40: Lath 3H 19

Daisy Wlk. PR8: South 2C 8
  (off Beacham Rd.)
Daisy Way PR8: South 1H 11
Dales Wlk. L37: Form 1F 15
DALTON 1H 25
Danbers WN8: Uph 3D 26
Daneway PR8: Ains 5B 10
Daniels La. WN8: Skel 6G 25
Daresbury Av. PR8: Ains 6A 10
Darfield WN8: Uph 2D 26
Dark La. L40: Lath 3H 21
Darwin Ct. PR9: South 6C 4
Davenham Rd. L39: Orm 3E 15
Dawlish Dr. PR9: Marsh 2E 5
Dawson Av. PR9: Cros 2G 5
Dawson Rd. L39: Orm 2F 21
Daybrook WN8: Uph 2D 26
Dayfield WN8: Uph 2E 27
Dean Cl. WN8: Uph 2G 27
Deans Ct. L37: Form 2E 15
Deansgate La. L37: Form 2G 15
Deansgate La. Nth. L37: Form 1F 15
Dearden Way WN8: Uph 2E 27
De-Haviland Way WN8: Skel 1C 26
Deighton Cl. WN5: Orr 4H 27
Delamere Rd. PR8: Ains 6B 10
  WN8: Skel .3D 24
Delamere Way WN8: Uph 2E 27
Delf Ho. WN8: Skel 4G 25
Dell, The WN8: Uph 2F 27
Delph Cl. L39: Augh 2E 23
Delph Comn. Rd. L39: Augh 2D 22
Delph Dr. L40: Burs 3F 19
Delph La. L37: Form 4B 14
  L39: Augh .2E 23
Delph Pk. Av. L39: Augh 2D 22
Delph Rd. L23: Lit C 6F 17
Delphside Cl. WN5: Orr 4H 27
Delphside Rd. WN5: Orr 4H 27
Delph Top L39: Orm 3G 21
Denbigh Av. PR9: Chu 4D 4
Denefield Ho. PR8: South 3H 7
  (off Portland St.)
Denholme WN8: Uph 2D 26
  (not continuous)
Denmark Rd. PR9: Chu 5E 5
Denshaw WN8: Uph 2D 26
Derby Ct. L37: Form 2D 14
Derby Hill Cres. L39: Orm 4G 21
Derby Hill Rd. L39: Orm 4G 21
Derby Ho. L39: Orm 4F 21
Derby Rd. L37: Form 2D 14
  PR9: South .2A 8
  WN8: Skel .5A 24
Derby St. L39: Orm 4F 21
Derby St. W. L39: Orm 4E 21
Derwent Av. L37: Form 5C 14
  PR9: Chu 6D 4
Devon Av. WN8: Uph 3F 27
Devon Farm Way L37: Form 4G 15
Devonshire Rd. PR9: South 1E 9
Dewberry Flds. WN8: Uph 2F 27
Dexter Way WN8: Uph 3F 27
Dicconson Way L39: Orm 5G 21
Dickinson Cl. L37: Form 5E 15
Dickinson Ct. PR8: B'dale 1G 11
Dickinson Rd. L37: Form 5E 15
DIGMOOR 3B 26
Digmoor Dr. WN8: Skel 6F 25
Digmoor Rd. WN8: Skel 6G 25
Dingle Av. WN8: Uph 1F 27
Dingle Cl. L39: Augh 2E 23
Dingle Rd. WN8: Uph 2F 27
Dinorwic Rd. PR8: B'dale 6G 7
Ditchfield L37: Form 5F 15
Dobbs Dr. L37: Form 3F 15
Dodworth Av. PR8: South 4C 8
Dolly's La. PR9: South 1H 9
Donnington Lodge PR8: South 3F 7
Dorchester Rd. WN8: Uph 2E 27
Doric Grn. WN5: Bil 6H 27
Dorset Av. PR8: Ains 3E 13
Douglas Av. WN8: Uph 2F 27
Douglas Dr. L39: Orm 2D 20

Douglas Rd. PR9: Cros 3G 5
Dover Rd. PR8: B'dale 1E 11
Downholland Moss La. L37: Form 3G 15
Dragon Cl. WN8: Skel 1C 26
Dragons Health Club 5A 4
Drake Cl. L39: Augh 1E 23
Drewitt Cres. PR9: Cros 3H 5
Duke Av. PR8: South 5A 8
Duke St. L37: Form 5D 14
  PR8: South 3G 7
Dukes Way L37: Form 5E 15
Duke's Wood La. WN8: Skel 6B 26
Dunbar Cres. PR8: B'dale 3F 11
Dunbar Rd. PR8: B'dale 1F 11
Dunes Dr. L37: Form 3B 14
Dunes Leisure Cen. 2F 7
Dunkirk Rd. PR8: B'dale 1F 11
Dunlop Av. L37: Ains 3E 13
Dunster Rd. PR8: B'dale 3E 11
Durham St. WN8: Skel 3B 24
Dyers La. L39: Orm 5E 21

E

Eamont Av. PR9: Marsh 2F 5
Earhart Cl. WN8: Skel 1C 26
Earlswood WN8: Skel 4H 25
Easby Cl. L37: Form 5F 15
Easedale Dr. PR8: Ains 1D 12
Eastbank Ho. PR8: South 3H 7
Eastbank St. PR8: South 2H 7
Eastbank St. Sq. PR8: South 2H 7
Eastbourne Rd. PR8: B'dale 6G 7
EAST GILLIBRANDS 5E 25
Eastleigh WN8: Skel 4H 25
East Mead L39: Augh 2D 22
EAST PIMBO 5D 26
East St. PR9: South 2B 8
Eavesdale WN8: Skel 1C 26
Eccles Rd. L37: Form 6C 14
Eden Av. PR9: Chu 4D 4
Edenfield Cl. PR8: South 6C 8
Edenhurst WN8: Skel 1C 26
Edenhurst Cl. L37: Form 5B 14
Edenhurst Dr. L37: Form 5B 14
Edge Hall Rd. WN5: Orr 5H 27
  (not continuous)
Edgley Dr. L39: Orm 4G 21
Edinburgh Rd. L37: Form 6D 14
Egerton WN8: Skel 5H 25
Eight Acre La. L37: Form 1F 15
Elbow La. L37: Form 4E 15
Elder Av. L40: Burs 4F 19
Eldons Cft. PR8: Ains 6D 10
Elizabeth Av. PR8: Ains 5E 11
Ellerbrook Dr. L40: Burs 4F 19
Ellerbrook Way L39: Orm 3E 21
Elm Ct. WN8: Skel 4C 24
Elmcroft La. L38: High 4C 16
Elmdale Cl. L37: Form 5C 14
Elm Dr. L37: Form 6C 14
ELMERS GREEN 4H 25
Elmers Grn. WN8: Skel 3H 25
  (not continuous)
Elmer's Grn. La. WN8: Dalt, Skel 2H 25
  WN8: Skel 1G 25
  (not continuous)
Elmers Wood Rd. WN8: Skel 4H 25
Elm Gro. WN8: Skel 4C 24
Elm Pk. Dr. PR8: Ains 6E 11
Elm Pl. L39: Orm 5E 21
Elmridge WN8: Skel 5H 25
Elm Rd. L40: Burs 4E 19
  PR8: South 5H 7
Elms, The PR8: South 4A 8
  (Ash St.)
  PR8: South 3F 7
  (Rotten Row)
Elmsfield Pk. L39: Augh 5C 22
Elmstead WN8: Skel 5H 25
Elmwood WN8: Skel 2G 25
Elson Rd. L37: Form 6C 14
Elswick WN8: Skel 5G 25

Elswick Grn. PR9: Marsh 2E 5
Elswick Rd. PR9: Marsh 3D 4
Elsworth Cl. L37: Form 6B 14
Elvington Rd. L38: High 5C 16
Ely M. PR9: Chu .5E 5
Emerson Cl. L38: High 3C 16
Emmanuel Rd. PR9: Chu 5D 4
Ennerdale WN8: Skel 5H 25
Ennerdale Cl. L37: Form 4C 14
Ennerdale Dr. L39: Augh 1D 22
Ennerdale Rd. L37: Form 4C 14
Enstone WN8: Skel 4H 25
Ericson Dr. PR8: South 4H 7
Eskbank WN8: Skel 5G 25
Eskbrook WN8: Skel 4G 25
Eskdale WN8: Skel 5F 25
Eskdale Av. L39: Augh 1D 22
Eskdale Cl. L37: Form 5C 14
Eskdale Dr. L37: Form 5C 14
Esplanade PR8: South 3E 7
Essex Rd. PR8: B'dale 3G 11
Eton Ct. PR9: South 6A 4
Ettington Dr. PR8: Ains 6A 10
Evenwood WN8: Skel 4H 25
Evenwood Ct. WN8: Skel 4G 25
Everard Rd. PR8: South 5B 8
Evergreens, The L37: Form 3C 14
Eversley WN8: Skel 4H 25
Everton Rd. PR8: B'dale 5G 7
Evington WN8: Skel 4H 25
Exmoor Cl. PR9: Marsh 1F 5

F

Fairburn WN8: Skel 2F 25
Fairfield Cl. L39: Orm 2E 21
Fairfield Dr. L39: Orm 2E 21
Fairfield Rd. PR8: Ains 6C 10
Fairhaven WN8: Skel 2F 25
Fairhaven Rd. PR9: Chu 3F 5
Fairlie WN8: Skel 2G 25
Fairstead WN8: Skel 2G 25
Fairway PR9: South 5A 4
Fairways, The WN8: Skel 2H 25
Fairways Ct. L37: Form 2B 14
Falkland WN8: Skel 2G 25
Falkland Rd. PR8: South 5B 8
Farm Cl. PR9: Chu 1E 9
Farm Mdw. Rd. WN5: Orr 4H 27
FAR MOOR 5H 27
Farnborough Rd. PR8: B'dale 3F 11
Farrington Dr. L39: Orm 3E 21
Faulkner Cl. PR8: Ains 6C 10
Faulkner Gdns. PR8: Ains 5C 10
Fawcett WN8: Skel 2F 25
Fell Vw. PR9: Cros 1H 5
Felstead WN8: Skel 3F 25
Feltons WN8: Skel 3F 25
Fenney Ct. WN8: Skel 4G 25
Fern Cl. WN8: Skel 4C 24
Ferndale WN8: Skel 3F 25
Fernhurst Ga. L39: Augh 1D 22
Fernley Rd. PR8: South 4G 7
Ferry Side La. PR9: Cros 2G 5
FIDDLER'S FERRY 1H 5
Field Cl. L40: Burs 4F 19
Field St. WN8: Skel 3B 24
Fieldview WN8: Uph 2E 27
Field Wlk. L39: Orm 4H 21
Findon WN8: Skel 3G 25
Fine Jane's Way PR9: Chu 1F 9
Firbeck WN8: Skel 4F 25
Firs Cl. L37: Form 2C 14
Firs Cres. L37: Form 2C 14
Firs La. L39: Augh 1A 22
Firs Link L37: Form 3C 14
Fir St. PR8: South 3C 8
Firswood Rd. WN8: Skel 3A 24
Fir Tree Cl. WN8: Skel 6H 25
Fir Tree La. L39: Augh, Hals 6A 20
Firwood WN8: Skel 2H 25
Fisher Dr. PR9: South 2D 8
Fishermans Cl. L37: Form 1D 14

Fisherman's Path L37: Form 6A 12
Flamstead WN8: Skel 4G 25
Flaxfield Rd. L37: Form 4F 15
Flaxfields L40: Lath 4F 19
Flax La. L40: Lath 4F 19
Flaxton WN8: Skel 4G 25
Fleetwood Cl. PR9: Chu 4D 4
Fleetwood Ct. PR9: South 6A 4
Fleetwood Rd. PR9: Chu, South 6A 4
  (not continuous)
Fletcher's Dr. L40: Burs 3E 19
Flimby WN8: Skel 4H 25
Floodgates Rd. L38: High 2B 16
Flordon WN8: Skel 4H 25
Folkestone Rd. PR8: South 6C 8
Fordham Cl. PR8: South 6C 8
Forest Dr. WN8: Skel 2G 25
Forest Rd. PR8: South 3B 8
FORMBY 4E 15
Formby Bri. L37: Form 5C 14
Formby Bus. Pk. L37: Form 5H 15
Formby By-Pass
  L37: Ains, Form, Ince B 6D 12
  L38: High 1D 16
Formby Flds. L37: Form 5F 15
Formby Gdns. L37: Form 3E 15
Formby Golf Course 1B 14
Formby La. L37: Form 5G 15
  L39: Augh 1A 22
Formby M. L37: Form 3E 15
Formby Point Cvn. Pk. L37: Form 6A 14
Formby Point Nature Reserve 6A 14
Formby Red Squirrel Reserve 2A 14
Formby Station (Rail) 5D 14
Formby St. L37: Form 5D 14
FORSTERS GREEN 2H 25
Forsters Grn. Rd. WN8: Skel 2H 25
Forum Ct. PR8: South 2G 7
Foster Rd. L37: Form 5C 14
Fosters Cl. PR9: Chu 1F 9
Foul La. PR8: South 5E 9
  PR9: South 4E 9
Fountains, The L39: Orm 3E 21
Fountains Way L37: Form 5F 15
Foxdale Cl. PR8: South 6C 8
Foxfold WN8: Skel 2H 25
Foxglove Av. L40: Burs 3F 19
Foxhill Cl. L37: Form 4B 14
Foxwood Cl. WN5: Orr 4H 27
Frailey Cl. PR8: Ains 1E 13
Freckleton Rd. PR9: Marsh 3D 4
FRESHFIELD 2D 14
Freshfield Cvn. Pk. L37: Form 1A 14
Freshfield Ct. L37: Form 3D 14
Freshfield Rd. L37: Form 2D 14
Freshfield Station (Rail) 2D 14
Friars Wlk. L37: Form 5G 15
Fulwood Av. PR8: South 5B 8
Funchal Av. L37: Form 6C 14
Furness Av. L37: Form 4E 15
  L39: Orm 5E 21
Furness Cl. PR8: Ains 2D 12
Furnival Dr. L40: Burs 3D 18
FX Leisure 2H 27
Fylde Rd. PR9: Cros, Chu, Marsh 3D 4
Fylde Rd. Ind. Est. PR9: Marsh 3E 5

G

Gable M. L37: Form 6F 15
Gainsborough Rd. PR8: B'dale 6E 7
Galleries, The L37: Form 4E 15
Galloway Rd. WN8: Uph 3F 27
Gantley Av. WN5: Bil 5H 27
Gantley Cres. WN5: Bil 6H 27
Gantley Rd. WN5: Bil 5H 27
Ganton Cl. PR8: South 6C 8
Garden Cotts. L39: Orm 4D 20
Gardiners Pl. WN8: Skel 5C 24
Gardner Rd. L39: Orm 5D 20
Garnett Grn. L39: Orm 5D 20
Garnett Pl. WN8: Skel 6E 25
Garrick Pde. PR8: South 2G 7

Garstang Rd. PR9: Marsh 3D 4
Gategill Gro. WN5: Bil 6H 27
Gaw Hill La. L39: Augh 6A 20
Gaw Hill Vw. L39: Augh 6B 20
George Dr. PR8: Ains 6E 11
George's Ter. WN5: Orr 4H 27
Georgian Pl. L37: Form 6D 14
Gerrard Pl. WN8: Skel 6D 24
Gilbert Pl. L40: Burs 3B 18
Gillibrands Rd. WN8: Skel 5D 24
Gladden Pl. WN8: Skel 5C 24
Gladstone Rd. PR9: South 3D 8
Glaisdale Dr. PR8: South 6D 8
Glamis Dr. PR9: Chu 4F 5
Glebe Pl. PR9: South 2H 7
Glebe Rd. WN8: Skel 5E 25
Glenburn Rd. WN8: Skel 1C 24
Glencoyne Dr. PR9: Marsh 1F 5
Glendale Way L37: Form 5E 15
Gleneagles Dr. PR8: Ains 2D 12
Glenmarsh Way L37: Form 4G 15
Glenpark Dr. PR9: Marsh 3F 5
Glenrose Ter. PR8: B'dale 4G 7
Glenroyd Dr. L40: Burs 3E 19
Gloucester Rd. PR8: B'dale 4F 7
GLOVERS BRIDGE 4F 19
Gordon Av. PR9: South 6A 4
Gordon M. PR9: South 6A 4
Gordon St. PR9: South 1H 7
Gordon Way PR9: South 1A 8
                              (off Gordon St.)
Gore Dr. L39: Augh 6E 21
Gores La. L37: Form 2D 14
Gorsefield L37: Form 1F 15
Gorse Way L37: Form 3B 14
Gorsey La. L38: High 6C 16
Gorsey Pl. WN8: Skel 6E 25
Gorst La. L40: Burs 2A 18
Gosforth Rd. PR9: South 1D 8
Gower Gdns. L40: Burs 4F 19
Gowery, The L37: Form 4F 15
Graburn Rd. L37: Form 3E 15
Grafton Dr. PR8: Ains 6A 10
Granby Cl. PR9: Chu 4D 4
Grange, The PR9: Chu 4G 5
Grange Av. PR9: South 1C 8
Grange La. L37: Form 2D 14
Grange Rd. L38: High 1A 16
  PR9: South 2C 8
Grantham Cl. PR8: B'dale 2G 11
Grantham Rd. PR8: B'dale 2G 11
Granton Cl. L37: Form 4D 14
Granville Cl. L39: Augh 2D 22
Granville Ct. PR9: South 6B 4
Granville Pk. L39: Augh 3D 22
Granville Pk. W. L39: Augh 3D 22
Granville Rd. PR8: B'dale 6D 6
Grasmere Av. WN8: Uph 2F 27
Grasmere Rd. L37: Form 4C 14
  L38: High 3C 16
Gratton Pl. WN8: Skel 5E 25
Graveyard La. L39: Bic 4H 23
Greenbank L39: Augh 1E 23
Greenbank Av. WN5: Bil 6H 27
Greenbank Dr. PR8: B'dale 1E 11
Greenfield Cl. PR9: South 4E 5
Greenford Cl. WN5: Orr 3H 27
Greenford Rd. PR8: Ains 1E 13
Greenhaven WN8: Uph 2F 27
Greenhey Pl. WN8: Skel 5D 24
Green La. L37: Form 2E 15
  L39: Orm 3E 21
  WN5: Bil 6H 27
Green La., The L40: Burs 3F 19
Green La. Av. L39: Orm 3E 21
Greenlea Cl. WN5: Orr 4H 27
Greenloons Dr. L37: Form 4B 14
Greenloon's Wlk. L37: Form 5B 14
Greenslate Ct. WN5: Bil 6H 27
                              (not continuous)
Greenslate Rd. WN5: Bil 6H 27
Green Wlk. PR8: Ains 6D 10
Greenway Av. WN8: Skel 6F 25
Greenway Cl. WN8: Skel 3C 24

Greenways WN5: Bil 6H 27
Greenwood Cl. L39: Augh 2E 23
Greenwood Gdns. PR8: B'dale 4G 7
Greetby Hill L39: Orm 4G 21
Greetby Pl. WN8: Skel 5E 25
Gregsons Av. L37: Form 2D 14
Greyfriars Rd. PR8: Ains 5B 10
Greystokes L39: Augh 1F 23
Griffiths Dr. PR9: South 1D 8
Grimrod Pl. WN8: Skel 6E 25
Grimshaw La. L39: Orm 3E 21
Grimshaw Rd. WN8: Skel 5E 25
Grinstead Cl. PR8: B'dale 2F 11
Grisedale Cl. L37: Form 4D 14
Grosvenor Cl. PR8: B'dale 6E 7
Grosvenor Gdns. PR8: B'dale 6F 7
Grosvenor Pl. PR8: B'dale 6F 7
Grosvenor Rd. PR8: B'dale 5D 6
Grove, The L39: Augh 4E 21
Grove Pk. L39: Orm 2F 21
  PR9: South 1D 8
Grove Rd. WN8: Uph 1G 27
Grove St. PR8: South 5G 7
Grove Ter. PR8: South 4G 7
Grovewood PR8: B'dale 4E 7
Grundy Cl. PR8: South 4C 8
Grundy Homes PR8: South 4C 8
Guardian Ct. PR8: B'dale 4F 7
Guildford Rd. PR8: B'dale 4F 11
Guys Ind. Est. L40: Burs 5B 18

H

Hadstock Av. L37: Form 6C 14
Haig Avenue 4C 8
Haig Av. PR8: South 4C 8
Haigh Ct. PR8: South 3D 8
Halifax Rd. PR8: Ains 6C 10
Hallbridge Gdns. WN8: Uph 1F 27
Hall Brow L39: Orm 5H 21
Hallcroft WN8: Skel 3G 25
HALL GREEN 2E 27
Hall Grn. WN8: Uph 2F 27
Hall Grn. Cl. WN8: Uph 2F 27
Hall La. L38: Ince B 3H 17
  L40: Lath 6G 19
Hallmoor Cl. L39: Augh 1G 23
Hall St. PR9: South 3A 8
Halsall Bldgs. PR9: South 2B 8
Halsall Cl. L39: Orm 3D 20
Halsall La. L37: Form 4E 15
  L39: Orm 3D 20
Halsall Rd. PR8: B'dale 3F 11
Hampton Rd. L37: Form 6D 14
  PR8: South 5H 7
Handsworth Wlk. PR8: South 6D 8
Hansby Cl. WN8: Skel 1C 26
Hanstock Cl. WN5: Orr 4H 27
Hants La. L39: Orm 3E 21
Harbury Av. PR8: Ains 1C 12
Hardacre St. L39: Orm 3F 21
Harding Rd. L40: Burs 3D 18
Harebell Cl. L37: Form 6E 15
Harewood Av. PR8: Ains 5C 10
Hargreaves St. PR8: South 3A 8
Harington Cl. L37: Form 4C 14
Harington Grn. L37: Form 4B 14
Harington Rd. L37: Form 2B 14
Harridge La. L40: Scar 1A 20
Harrier Dr. WN8: Skel 1C 26
Harrod Dr. PR8: B'dale 6E 7
Harrogate Way PR9: Cros 1G 5
Harsnips WN8: Skel 3G 25
Harswell Cl. WN5: Orr 4H 27
Hartland WN8: Skel 3G 25
Hartland Av. PR9: Marsh 2F 5
Hartley Cres. PR8: B'dale 1F 11
Hartley Rd. PR8: B'dale 1F 11
Hartshead WN8: Skel 3G 25
Hart's La. WN8: Uph 1D 26
Hart St. PR8: South 3B 8
Hart St. Bri. PR8: South 3B 8
                              (off Hart St.)

Hartwood Rd. PR9: South 2B 8
Harvington Dr. PR8: Ains 6A 10
Haslam Dr. L39: Orm 2D 20
Hastings Rd. PR8: B'dale 1E 11
Hatfield Rd. PR8: Ains 5C 10
Haven Brow L39: Augh 3E 23
Hawesside St. PR9: South 2A 8
Hawker Dr. WN8: Skel 1C 26
Hawksclough WN8: Skel 3G 25
Hawkshead St. PR8: South 2C 8
  PR9: South 1A 8
Hawksworth Cl. L37: Form 1F 15
Hawksworth Dr. L37: Form 1F 15
Hawthorn Cres. WN8: Skel 4C 24
Hawthorne Av. L40: Burs 3F 19
Hawthorne Cres. L37: Form 5F 15
Hawthorne Gro. PR9: South 2D 8
Hayfield Rd. L39: Orm 2E 21
Haylemere Ct. PR8: B'dale 4E 7
Hayward Ct. L37: Form 3F 15
Hazelbank Gdns. L37: Form 2D 14
Hazel Gro. PR8: South 2C 8
Hazelhurst Cl. L37: Form 5B 14
Hazel La. WN8: Skel 1F 25
Hazelwood Av. L40: Burs 3E 19
Headbolt La. PR8: Ains 1H 13
  PR8: B'dale 5G 11
                              (not continuous)
Headingly Av. WN8: Skel 3A 24
Heanor Dr. PR8: South 6D 8
Heap Ct. PR9: South 1C 8
Heather Cl. L37: Form 2G 15
  L40: Burs 3E 19
  PR8: Ains 3F 13
Heatherlea Cl. WN8: Uph 2G 27
Heatherways L37: Form 2F 15
Heathfield L40: Burs 3F 19
Heathfield Cl. L37: Form 1F 15
Heathfield Rd. PR8: Ains 5E 11
Heathgate WN8: Skel 3G 25
Heathland WN8: Uph 2F 27
Heaton Cl. L40: Burs 3D 18
  WN8: Uph 2E 27
Helmsdale WN8: Skel 2G 25
Helston Cl. PR9: Marsh 2F 5
Henley Ct. PR9: South 6C 4
Henley Dr. PR9: South 6D 4
Hereford Gro. WN8: Uph 3F 27
Hereford Rd. PR9: South 2D 8
HESKETH CENTRE, THE 6A 4
Hesketh Dr. PR9: South 5C 4
Hesketh Links Ct. PR9: Chu 5C 4
Hesketh Mnr. PR9: Chu 5C 4
Hesketh Rd. L40: Burs 3D 18
  PR9: South 4B 4
Hesketh Vw. PR9: South 6C 4
Heskin La. L39: Orm 1D 20
Hester Cl. L38: High 3B 16
Heversham WN8: Skel 3G 25
Heydon Cl. L37: Form 6C 14
Heyes Rd. WN5: Orr 3H 27
Heys, The PR8: B'dale 5D 6
Heysham Rd. PR9: South 2D 8
Heywood Cl. L37: Form 4D 14
Higgins La. L40: Burs 2B 18
HIGHER END 6H 27
Higher La. WN8: Dalt 1G 25
  WN8: Uph 2G 27
Higher Vw. WN8: Uph 3G 27
Highfield Rd. L39: Orm 2E 21
  PR9: Chu 4F 5
Highgate Rd. WN8: Uph 2F 27
High La. L40: Burs 2G 19
Highmeadow WN8: Uph 3E 27
High Moss L39: Orm 6D 20
HIGH PARK 1E 9
High Pk. Pl. PR9: Chu, South 1E 9
High Pk. Rd. PR9: South 1E 9
High St. WN8: Skel 5B 24
HIGHTOWN 3B 16
Hightown Station (Rail) 3B 16
Hilary Ct. L37: Form 5D 14
Hilbre Cl. PR9: South 6D 4
Hilbre Dr. PR9: South 6D 4

Hillcrest WN8: Skel	Ivydale WN8: Skel	Lady Grn. Ct. L38: Ince B
...........6F 25	...........3F 25	...........4G 17
Hillcrest Rd. L39: Orm 3E 21	Ivy St. PR8: South 3B 8	Lady Grn. La. L38: Ince B 3F 17
Hilldean WN8: Uph 1G 27		Lady's Wlk. L40: Westh 4H 21
Hill Rise Vw.		Lafford La. WN8: Uph 1G 27
L39: Augh 2C 22		LA Fitness
HILLSIDE 2E 11	**J**	Formby 6F 15
Hillside Av. L39: Orm 5D 20		Lakes Dr. WN5: Orr 3H 27
Hillside Golf Course 3D 10	Jane's Brook Rd. PR8: South 5B 8	Lakeside Av. WN5: Bil 6H 27
Hillside Rd. PR8: B'dale 2E 11	Johnson St. PR9: South 1H 7	Lakeview Ct. PR9: South 1H 7
Hillside Station (Rail) 2E 11	Jubilee Av. L39: Orm 3F 21	Lambourne WN8: Skel 1F 25
Hill St. PR9: South 1H 7	WN5: Orr 5H 27	Lancaster Cl. PR8: B'dale 5E 7
Hillsview Rd. PR8: Ains 1E 13	Jubilee Ct. PR9: Chu 1E 9	Lancaster Cres. WN8: Skel 4C 24
Hilltop Wlk. L39: Orm 6C 20	Jubilee Dr. WN8: Skel 5C 24	Lancaster Gdns. PR8: B'dale 5E 7
Hobberley Dr. WN8: Skel 1C 26	Jubilee Ho. L37: Form 5H 15	Lancaster Rd. L37: Form 6D 14
Hobcross La. L40: Lath 6G 19	Jubilee Rd. L37: Form 6C 14	PR8: B'dale 6D 6
Hodge St. PR8: South 2H 7	Junction La. L40: Burs 3E 19	Land La. PR9: Cros 3H 5
Hodson St. PR8: South 3A 8		Langdale Av. L37: Form 5C 14
Hoggs Hill La. L37: Form 6D 14		Langdale Cl. L37: Form 5C 14
Hoghton Gro.	**K**	Langdale Dr. L40: Burs 3E 19
PR9: South 1A 8		Langdale Gdns. PR8: B'dale 2F 11
Hoghton Pl. PR9: South 2H 7	Kart World 5B 18	Langley Brook Rd. L40: Burs 3B 18
Hoghton St. PR9: South 2H 7	Keats Ter. PR8: South 3D 8	Langley Cl. L38: High 5B 16
Holborn Dr. L39: Orm 6C 20	Kempton Pk. Fold PR8: South 6D 8	Langley Ct. L40: Burs 2B 18
Holborn Hill L39: Orm 6C 20	Kendal Way PR8: Ains 2D 12	Langley Pl. L40: Burs 3B 18
Holgate Dr. WN5: Orr 3H 27	Kenilworth Rd. PR8: Ains 6B 10	Langley Rd. L40: Burs 2B 18
Holland Bus. Pk. L40: Lath 1A 24	Kensington Ct. L37: Form 4F 15	Langtree WN8: Skel 2F 25
HOLLAND MOOR 2C 26	Kensington Ind. Est. PR9: South 3A 8	Lansdowne Rd. PR8: South 3C 8
Hollies, The L39: Augh 5A 20	Kensington Rd. L37: Form 6D 14	Larch Cl. WN8: Skel 4C 24
PR8: South 3F 7	PR9: South 2A 8	Larch St. PR8: South 4C 8
(off Beechfield Gdns.)	Kent Av. L37: Form 6F 15	Larch Way L37: Form 3C 14
Hollowford La. L40: Lath 4H 19	Kenton Cl. L37: Form 1E 15	Larkfield Ct. PR9: Chu 4E 5
Hollybrook Rd. PR8: South 4G 7	Kent Rd. L37: Form 6E 15	Larkfield La. PR9: Chu 4E 5
Holly Cl. WN8: Skel 4C 24	PR8: B'dale 5G 7	Larkhill WN8: Skel 1F 25
Holly La. L39: Augh 5B 20	Kenworthy's Flats PR9: South 1H 7	Larkhill Gro. L38: High 4B 16
Holmdale Av. PR9: Cros 3F 5	Kenyons La. L37: Form 4F 15	Larkhill La. L37: Form 3B 14
Holmfield Pk. L37: Form 3D 14	Kerfoots La. WN8: Skel 5A 24	Larkspur Cl. PR8: South 3B 8
Holmwood Cl. L37: Form 4C 14	Kerslake Way L38: High 3B 16	Latham Av. L39: Orm 4G 21
Holmwood Dr. L37: Form 3C 14	Kerton Row PR8: B'dale 5F 7	LATHOM 5G 19
Holmwood Gdns. L37: Form 3C 14	Kestrel Ct. PR9: South 2B 8	Lathom Cl. L40: Burs 3E 19
Holt Coppice L39: Augh 4C 22	Kestrel M. WN8: Skel 1G 25	Lathom Ho. L40: Burs 3E 19
HOLT GREEN 5D 22	Kestrel Pk. WN8: Skel 1G 25	Lathom Rd. PR9: South 6A 4
Holt St. WN5: Orr 4H 27	Keswick Cl. PR8: Ains 2E 13	Laurel Av. L40: Burs 1E 19
Homechase Ho. PR8: B'dale 5F 7	Kettering Rd. PR8: Ains 6B 10	Laurel Dr. WN8: Skel 3C 24
Homeport Ho. PR9: South 1A 8	KEW 6C 8	Laurel Gro. PR8: South 2C 8
(off Hoghton St.)	Kew Retail Pk. PR8: South 5E 9	Lawns, The PR9: Chu 5D 4
Homesands Ho. PR9: South 1B 8	Kew Rd. L37: Form 6C 14	Lawns Av. WN5: Orr 4G 27
Hope Sq. PR9: South 2A 8	PR8: B'dale 6G 7	Lawson St. PR9: South 2E 9
Hope St. PR9: South 2A 8	Kilburn Rd. WN5: Orr 4G 27	Lawswood L37: Form 2D 14
Hornby Rd. PR9: Marsh 2E 5	Killingbeck Cl. L40: Burs 3D 18	Lea Cres. L39: Orm 2E 21
Hoscar Moss Rd. L40: Lath 4H 19	Kiln La. WN8: Skel 3C 24	Leamington Av. PR8: Ains 6D 10
Houghton's La. WN8: Skel 4G 25	Kingfisher Ct. PR9: South 1B 8	Leamington Rd. PR8: Ains 6C 10
(not continuous)	Kingfisher Pk. WN8: Skel 1G 25	Ledburn WN8: Skel 2F 25
Houghtons Rd. WN8: Skel 2E 25	Kingsbury Cl. PR8: Ains 1D 12	Ledson Gro. L39: Augh 4D 22
Howard Ct. PR9: South 6B 4	Kingsbury Ct. WN8: Skel 1G 25	Leeswood WN8: Skel 2F 25
Hulme St. PR9: South 2G 7	Kings Cl. L37: Form 5D 14	Leicester St. PR9: South 6A 4
Hunts Cotts. PR9: Chu 6E 5	Kings Hey Dr. PR9: Chu 6D 4	Lendel Cl. L37: Form 4D 14
Hurlston Av. WN8: Skel 5G 25	Kings Mdw. PR8: Ains 2F 13	Lenton Av. L37: Form 3C 14
Hurlston Dr. L39: Orm 2E 21	Kings Rd. L37: Form 5D 14	Lesley Rd. PR8: South 2C 8
Hurstwood L37: Form 2D 14	Kingston Cres. PR9: Cros 2G 5	Lethbridge Rd. PR8: South 4B 8
Hutton Ct. WN8: Skel 4B 24	King St. PR8: South 3G 7	Lexton Dr. PR9: Chu 4F 5
Hutton Rd. WN8: Skel 4B 24	Kingsway PR8: South 2G 7	Leybourne Av. PR8: Ains 4F 11
Hutton Way L39: Orm 4E 21	Kingswood Ho. PR8: B'dale 4F 7	Leyland Mans. PR9: South 1B 8
Hythe Cl. PR8: South 6C 8	Kingswood Pk. PR8: B'dale 4F 7	Leyland Rd. PR9: South 6A 4
	Kingswood Pk. M. PR8: B'dale 3F 7	Leyland Way L39: Orm 4F 21
	Kinloch Way L39: Orm 4D 20	Lifeboat Rd. L37: Form 6A 14
I	Kirkdale Gdns. WN8: Uph 2E 27	Lighthorne Dr. PR8: Ains 1C 12
	Kirkham Rd. PR9: Chu 3E 5	Lilac Av. PR8: Ains 3F 13
Ilkley Av. PR9: Cros 1G 5	Kirklake Bank L37: Form 5B 14	Lilac Gro. WN8: Skel 4C 24
INCE BLUNDELL 4G 17	Kirklake Rd. L37: Form 5B 14	Lime Cl. WN8: Skel 4C 24
INCE Cres. L37: Form 4C 14	Kirklees Rd. PR8: B'dale 2F 11	Limefield Dr. WN8: Skel 2C 24
Ince La. L23: Thorn 6H 17	Kirkstall Dr. L37: Form 5G 15	Lime Gro. WN8: Skel 4B 24
Inchfield WN8: Skel 3F 25	Kirkstall Rd. PR8: B'dale 1F 11	Lime St. PR8: South 3C 8
Ingleton Rd. PR8: South 6C 8	Knob Hall Gdns. PR9: Chu 4D 4	Lime Tree Way L37: Form 5B 14
Inglewhite WN8: Skel 3E 25	Knob Hall La. PR9: Chu 4D 4	Limont Rd. PR8: Ains 6D 10
Ingram WN8: Skel 4F 25	Knowle Av. PR8: Ains 5B 10	Linaker St. PR8: South 4H 7
Inskip WN8: Skel 3E 25	Knowsley Rd. L39: Orm 5F 21	Lincoln Rd. PR8: B'dale 2G 11
Inskip Ct. WN8: Skel 3F 25	PR9: South 6A 4	Lindens WN8: Skel 2F 25
Inskip Rd. PR9: Marsh 3E 5		Linden Wlk. WN5: Orr 3H 27
Irton Rd. PR9: South 1C 8		Lindholme WN8: Skel 2G 25
Irvin Av. PR9: Cros 2G 5	**L**	Lindley Av. WN5: Orr 4G 27
Irving St. PR9: South 6A 4		Lingdales L37: Form 1G 15
Irwell Rd. PR8: South 2E 25	Laburnum Dr. WN8: Skel 4B 24	Links Av. PR9: Chu 5C 4
Ivybridge WN8: Skel 3F 25	Laburnum Gro. L40: Burs 1E 19	Lismore Pk. PR8: B'dale 5E 7
Ivy Cl. L40: Burs 4G 19	PR8: South 2D 8	LITTLE ALTCAR 6F 15
	LADY GREEN 3F 17	

Lit. Brewery La. L37: Form 1E 15
Lit. Hey La. L37: Form 3G 15
Little La. PR9: Chu 5F 5
Little Theatre 2H 7
Liverpool Av. PR8: Ains 6D 10
Liverpool Rd. L31: Lyd 6A 22
    L37: Form .5F 15
    L39: Augh .1D 22
    L39: Bic 6H 23
    PR8: Ains 3E 13
    PR8: B'dale .5G 7
    WN8: Skel .5A 24
                                    (not continuous)
Liverpool Rd. Nth. L40: Burs 3E 19
Liverpool Rd. Sth. L40: Burs 6B 18
Lodge Rd. WN5: Orr 5H 27
London Sq. PR9: South 2H 7
London St. PR9: South 2H 7
Longacre PR9: Chu 4D 4
Longcliffe Dr. PR8: Ains 1D 12
Longfield L37: Form 2G 15
Longford Rd. PR8: B'dale 1G 11
Longhey WN8: Skel 1G 25
Long Heys La. WN8: Dalt 1H 25
Long La. L37: Form 3D 14
    L39: Augh, Bic 6C 20
    WN8: Uph .6C 26
Longton Ct. PR9: South 1B 8
Longton Dr. L37: Form 1F 15
Lonsdale Av. L39: Orm 2F 21
Lonsdale Rd. L37: Form 4D 14
    PR8: South 5B 8
Lord Sefton Way L37: Gt Alt 5H 15
Lordsgate Dr. L40: Burs 4E 19
Lordsgate La. L40: Burs 5C 18
Lord St. L40: Burs 2E 19
    PR8: South .3G 7
    PR9: South .3G 7
Lord St. W. PR8: South 3G 7
Loves Cotts. L39: Orm 3D 20
Lowcroft WN8: Skel 2G 25
Lwr. Alt Rd. L38: High 3B 16
Lwr. Promenade PR8: South 2G 7
    PR9: South .1H 7
Lowes Grn. L37: Form 4G 15
Lowry Hill La. L40: Lath 5H 19
Low Wood L38: High 1B 16
Loxley Rd. PR8: South 5B 8
Ludlow WN8: Skel 1G 25
Ludlow Dr. L39: Orm 2D 20
Lulworth WN8: Skel 1F 25
Lulworth Lodge PR8: B'dale 4F 7
Lulworth Rd. PR8: B'dale 5E 7
Lulworth Vw. PR8: B'dale 5E 7
Lunt's La. L37: Form 6F 15
Lynbridge Cl. WN5: Orr 4H 27
Lyndale WN8: Skel 1F 25
Lyndhurst WN8: Skel 1F 25
Lyndhurst Rd. PR8: B'dale 1G 11
Lynton Dr. PR8: B'dale 2E 11
Lynton Rd. PR8: B'dale 3E 11
Lynwood Av. L39: Augh 6C 20
Lynwood Cl. WN8: Skel 6H 25
Lynwood End L39: Augh 6C 20
Lyons Rd. PR8: B'dale 4G 7
Lytham Rd. PR9: Chu 3E 5
Lytles Cl. L37: Form 5F 15

M

Madingley Ct. PR9: Chu 5D 4
Maiden Cl. WN8: Skel 3A 24
Majestic M. WN5: Orr 4H 27
Malham Cl. PR8: South 6C 8
Mall, The L39: Orm 4F 21
Mallard Cl. L39: Augh 1E 23
Mallards, The PR9: Cros 4G 5
Mallee Av. PR9: Chu 4E 5
Mallee Cres. PR9: Chu 4E 5
Maltkiln La. L39: Augh 2G 23
Malvern Cl. PR8: South 3G 7
Malvern Gdns. PR8: South 3G 7
Manchester Rd. PR9: South 1A 8

Mandeville Rd. PR8: Ains 6B 10
Manfield WN8: Skel 2E 25
Manning Rd. PR8: South 3C 8
Manor Av. L40: Burs 5D 18
Manor Ct. PR9: Chu 5E 5
Manor Cres. L40: Burs 5D 18
Manor Dr. L40: Burs 5D 18
Manor Gdns. L40: Burs 5D 18
Manor Gro. WN8: Skel 4D 24
Manor Ho. Dr. WN8: Skel 6C 26
Manor Lodge L37: Form 3D 14
Manor Rd. L40: Burs 5D 18
    PR9: Chu 5E 5
Manx Jane's La. PR9: Chu 3E 5
Maple Av. L40: Burs 3E 19
Maple Cl. L37: Form 6B 14
Maple St. PR8: South 3C 8
Maple Vw. WN8: Skel 6D 24
Maplewood PR9: Chu 5D 4
    WN8: Skel .1E 25
Marble Pl. Shop. Cen. PR8: South 2H 7
Marchbank Rd. WN8: Skel 4B 24
Mardale Cl. PR8: Ains 1D 12
Marians Dr. L39: Orm 1E 21
Marina Rd. L37: Form 6E 15
Marine Dr. PR8: South . . . . .2F 7 & 5A 4
    PR9: Cros, Chu, Marsh, South
    . . . . .4A 4 & 1F 5
Marine Ga. Mans. PR9: South 1H 7
Mariner Cl. PR9: South 6A 4
Marine Rd. PR8: South 3E 7
Marine Way PR8: South 1G 7
Maritime Ct. PR8: South 2H 7
Market St. PR8: South 2G 7
Market Way L39: Orm 4E 21
Markham Dr. PR8: South 6C 8
Mark Rd. L38: High 3B 16
Marland WN8: Skel 1E 25
Marlborough WN8: Skel 1E 25
Marlborough Ct. PR9: South 2A 8
    WN8: Skel .1E 25
Marlborough Gdns. PR9: South 1A 8
    WN8: Skel .1E 25
Marlborough Rd. PR9: South 2A 8
Marlborough Ter. PR9: South 2A 8
                            (off Marlborough Rd.)
Marl Gro. WN5: Orr 5H 27
Marsden Rd. PR9: South 2C 8
Marshallsay L37: Form 5F 15
Marsh Brows L37: Form 5D 14
Marsh La. L38: Ince B 1E 17
    L40: Scar .1D 20
MARSHSIDE 4E 5
Marshside Rd. PR9: Chu 2C 4
Marshside Sands Nature Reserve 2A 4
Marston Cres. L38: High 5C 16
Martin La. : Burs 2A 18
Martins La. L37: Form 6H 25
Mart La. L40: Burs 2E 19
Mary Av. PR8: Ains 5E 11
Massam's La. L37: Form 1D 14
Matlock Av. PR8: South 5H 7
Matlock Cl. PR8: South 5H 7
Matlock Cres. PR8: South 5H 7
Matlock Rd. PR8: B'dale 6H 7
Mawdsley Cl. L37: Form 4G 15
Mawdsley Ter. L39: Orm 1F 21
Maybank Cl. PR9: Chu 6E 5
Mayfair Cl. L38: High 5B 16
Mayfield Av. L37: Form 6B 14
Mayfield Ct. L37: Form 2D 14
Mayfield Rd. WN8: Uph 2E 27
                                    (not continuous)
Mayflower Ind. Est. L37: Form 6F 15
Maytree Wlk. WN8: Skel 1F 25
Meadow Av. PR8: South 5A 8
Meadow Bank L39: Orm 5F 21
Meadow Brook L40: Burs 4D 18
Meadow Brow PR9: Cros 2H 5
Meadow Cl. WN8: Skel 6H 25
Meadow Clough WN8: Skel 1F 25
Meadowcroft L37: Form 5E 15
    WN8: Skel .1F 25
Meadow Dr. L39: Augh 1E 23

Meadowfield WN8: Uph 2E 27
Meadow La. L40: Lath 4H 19
    PR8: Ains 2E 13
Meadow Vw. PR8: South 5B 8
Meadway WN8: Skel 1F 25
Mecca Bingo
    Southport 2G 7
Melbreck WN8: Skel 1E 25
Meldreth Cl. L37: Form 6B 14
Melford Dr. WN5: Bil 6H 27
Melling Rd. PR9: South 1C 8
Mellors Cl. PR8: South 4D 8
Melrose Av. PR9: Marsh 2F 5
Melvin Ho. PR9: South 1H 7
Menivale Cl. PR9: Marsh 1F 5
Meols Cl. L37: Form 5D 14
Meols Cop Retail Pk. PR8: South 5D 8
Meols Cop Rd. PR8: South 4D 8
Meols Cop Station (Rail) 2D 8
Meols Hall 6F 5
Meols Vw. Cl. PR8: South 6E 9
Mercury Way WN8: Skel 1C 26
Mere Av. L40: Burs 1E 19
Mere Cl. WN8: Skel 3D 24
Mere Ct. L40: Burs 1E 19
Mereland Cl. WN5: Orr 3H 27
Merepark Dr. PR9: Marsh 3F 5
Mere Rd. L37: Form 5C 14
Meres Way PR8: South 1H 11
Merewood WN8: Skel 1E 25
Meriden Cl. PR8: Ains 1D 12
Merlewood Av. PR9: Chu 4F 5
Mersey Av. L37: Form 1D 14
Mews, The PR8: South 4G 7
Michaels Cl. L37: Form 4D 14
Mickering La. L39: Augh 5D 22
Mickleton Dr. PR8: South 6A 10
Middlecot Cl. WN5: Orr 4H 27
Middlewood WN8: Skel 1E 25
Middlewood Cl. L39: Augh 4E 23
Middlewood Dr. L39: Augh 4E 23
Middlewood Rd. L39: Augh 3E 23
Midhurst Dr. PR8: Ains 1D 12
Midhurst Dr. PR8: Ains 1D 12
Milford Cl. L37: Form 6B 14
Millar's Pace PR9: Marsh 2F 5
Millbank Brow L40: Burs 4F 19
Millbrook PR8: South 5H 7
Millbrook Cl. WN8: Skel 3C 24
Millcroft Av. WN5: Orr 4H 27
Mill Dam Cl. L40: Burs 5C 18
Mill Dam La. L40: Burs 5C 18
Millers Ct. L39: Orm 4F 21
Millers Nook WN8: Uph 2F 27
Mill Gdns. L39: Orm 4F 21
Millgreen Cl. WN8: Uph 2E 27
Mill Ho. Lodge PR8: Ains 6D 10
Mill Ho. Vw. WN8: Uph 2G 27
Mill La. L39: Augh 2B 22
    L40: Burs 3E 19
                                        (Junction La.)
    L40: Burs 6E 5
                                    (Liverpool Rd. N.)
    PR9: Chu 6E 5
    WN8: Dalt, Uph 1E 27
Mill La. Cres. PR9: Chu 6E 5
Mill Rd. PR8: Ains 6D 10
    WN5: Orr .4H 27
Millrose Cl. WN8: Skel 3D 24
Mill St. L39: Orm 5F 21
    PR8: South 3A 8
Milman Cl. L39: Orm 6D 20
Milton Dr. L37: Form 5G 21
Milton St. PR9: South 2D 8
Mitten's La. L37: Form 3F 15
Model Railway Village 2G 7
Molyneux Rd. L39: Augh 4E 23
Monks Carr La. L38: Gt Alt 1H 17
Monks Cl. L37: Form 6F 15
Monks Dr. L37: Form 6F 15
Monk's La. L40: Burs 1D 18
Montagu M. L37: Form 2D 14
Montagu Rd. L37: Form 1D 14
Montgomery Av. PR9: South 3E 9
Montrose Dr. PR9: Chu 6D 4

Moor Cl. PR8: Ains 3E 13
Moor Dr. WN8: Skel 6H 25
Moorgate L39: Orm 5E 21
Moor La. L38: Ince B 3F 17
   PR8: Ains .3E 13
Moor Rd. WN5: Orr 4H 27
Moor St. L39: Orm 4E 21
   (not continuous)
Morley Rd. PR9: South 6C 4
Mornington Rd. PR9: South 2A 8
Morris Rd. WN8: Skel 2E 27
Morven Gro. PR8: South 2C 8
Mosley St. PR8: South 5H 7
Moss Av. WN5: Bil 6H 27
Moss Bank L39: Augh 1F 23
Moss Bank Ct. L39: Augh 1F 23
   (not continuous)
Moss Delph La. L39: Augh 1D 22
Mossgiel Av. PR8: Ains 1D 12
Moss Grn. L37: Form 4F 15
Moss La. L23: Lit C 3E 17
   L31: Lyd 6A 22
   L38: High .2C 16
   L40: Burs .1F 19
   PR9: Chu 1E 9
   PR9: South 1H 9
   WN8: Skel . . . . .6D 24 & 6E 25
Moss La. Vw. WN8: Skel 6D 24
Moss Nook L39: Augh 1E 23
   L40: Burs .1E 19
Moss Rd. PR8: South 1H 11
   WN5: Bil 6H 27
Moss Side L37: Form 3G 15
Moss Vw. L39: Orm 5E 21
Motherwell Cres. PR8: South 6D 8
Mount, The WN8: Skel 5F 25
Mount Ho. Cl. L37: Form 2G 15
Mount Ho. Rd. L37: Form 2G 15
Mount St. PR9: South 2B 8
Mount Ter. PR9: South 2B 8
Mountwood WN8: Skel 1E 25
Mountwood Lodge PR8: Ains 6C 10
Muirfield Dr. PR8: Ains 1E 13
Mullion Cl. PR9: Marsh 2F 5
Munro Av. WN5: Orr 3H 27
Myrtle Gro. PR8: South 3C 8
Mystic M. L39: Orm 4E 21
   (off Burscough St.)

N

Naburn Dr. WN5: Orr 4H 27
Nairn Av. WN8: Skel 1F 25
Napier Ter. PR8: B'dale 4G 7
Narrow Cft. Rd. L39: Augh 2D 22
Narrow La. L39: Augh 2D 22
NARROW MOSS 1E 21
Narrow Moss La. L40: Scar 1E 21
Neales Fold PR9: Cros 2H 5
Needham Way WN8: Skel 1F 25
Nell's La. L39: Augh 6B 22
Nelson Ct. PR8: B'dale 5F 7
Nelson St. PR8: South 3G 7
Neverstitch Cl. WN8: Skel 3D 24
Neverstitch Rd. WN8: Skel 4A 24
Nevill St. PR9: South 1H 7
Newburn Cl. WN8: Skel 1F 25
Newbury Rd. WN8: Skel 1F 25
Newby Cl. PR8: Ains 2D 12
Newby Dr. WN8: Skel 1F 25
New C'way. L37: Gt Alt 6G 15
New Ct. Way L39: Orm 4F 21
New Cut Cl. PR8: B'dale 3G 11
New Cut La. PR8: B'dale 3G 11
New Fold WN5: Orr 5G 27
New Foul La. PR8: South 5E 9
NEWGATE .2E 27
Newgate Rd. WN8: Uph 2D 26
Newlands Av. L40: Burs 3F 19
NEW LANE .1B 18
New La. L39: Augh 1G 23
   L40: Burs .1B 18
   PR9: Cros .3G 5

New Lane Station (Rail) 1B 18
Newlyn Dr. WN8: Skel 6H 25
New Rd. L37: Form 2F 15
Newstead Dr. WN8: Skel 1F 25
Newton Dr. WN8: Skel 1F 25
Newton St. PR9: South 2D 8
Nipe La. WN8: Skel 4A 26
Nixons La. PR8: Ains 4E 11
   WN8: Skel .6H 25
Noel Ga. L39: Augh 2D 22
Nolan St. PR8: South 4A 8
Nook, The L39: Augh 3E 23
Norburn Cres. L37: Form 5E 15
Norbury Cl. PR9: Cros 2G 5
Norfield L39: Orm 4F 21
Norfolk Gro. PR8: B'dale 2F 11
Norfolk Rd. PR8: B'dale 2F 11
Norman Hays L39: Orm 1F 21
Normanhurst L39: Orm 5G 21
Norris Ho. Dr. L39: Augh 3E 23
Norris Way L37: Form 4G 15
Northam Cl. PR9: Marsh 2E 5
NORTH END 1E 17
North End La. L38: High 1C 16
Northfield WN8: Skel 1F 25
Northleach Dr. PR8: Ains 6A 10
Nth. Moss La. L37: Form 1H 15
North Rd. PR9: Cros 3F 5
North St. PR9: South 1A 8
Northway L39: Augh 6A 22
   WN8: Skel .2F 25
Norwood Av. PR9: South 1C 8
Norwood Cres. PR9: South 1C 8
Norwood Gdns. PR9: South 2D 8
Norwood Rd. PR8: South 2D 8
Nurseries, The L37: Form 5F 15
Nursery Av. L39: Orm 3G 21
Nursery Dr. L37: Form 5E 15
Nuthall Rd. PR8: South 6D 8
Nye Bevan Pool 4F 25

O

Oak Av. L39: Orm 5D 20
Oak Cres. WN8: Skel 4B 24
Oak Dr. L40: Burs 4F 19
Oakfield Dr. L37: Form 3C 14
Oakfield Rd. L38: High 5B 16
Oakfields L39: Orm 4G 21
Oak Grn. L39: Orm 4F 21
Oakham Ct. PR9: South 1A 8
Oak St. PR8: South 3C 8
Oak Tree Ct. WN8: Skel 2H 25
Oakwood WN8: Skel 2H 25
Oakwood Av. PR8: Ains 5D 10
Oakwood Dr. PR8: Ains 6E 11
Ocean Plaza PR8: South 1G 7
Off Botanic Rd. PR9: Chu 6E 5
Old Acre L38: High 4B 16
Old Boundary Way L39: Orm 3F 21
Old Engine La. WN8: Skel 3A 24
Old Hall Farm Bus. Pk. PR9: South 4E 9
Old La. L31: Lyd 6A 22
   L37: Form .1E 15
Old Links Cl. PR9: Chu 1F 9
Old Mill Hill L39: Orm 6D 20
Old Mill La. L37: Form 3E 15
Old Pk. La. PR9: South 2E 9
Old Rectory Grn. L39: Augh 4C 22
Old Town Cl. WN8: Skel 5B 24
Old Town Ct. L37: Form 3D 14
Old Town La. L37: Form 3D 14
Old Town Way WN8: Skel 5B 24
Olive Gro. PR8: South 2C 8
   WN8: Skel .4C 24
Onslow Cres. PR8: B'dale 1G 11
Orchard, The L39: Orm 4D 20
Orchard Cl. WN5: Bil 6H 27
Orchard La. PR8: Ains 1F 13
Orchards, The PR8: Ains 1F 13
Orchard Vw. L39: Augh 2F 23
Orchid Cl. WN8: Uph 3F 27

Orme Ho. L39: Orm 4G 21
ORMSKIRK .4E 21
ORMSKIRK AND DISTRICT
   GENERAL HOSPITAL 5G 21
Ormskirk Bus. Pk. L39: Orm 3F 21
Ormskirk Civic Hall 3E 21
Ormskirk Rd. WN8: Skel 4A 24
   (Blaguegate La.)
   WN8: Skel .5F 25
   (Spencers La.)
   WN8: Uph .2D 26
Ormskirk Station (Rail) 4F 21
Orms Way L37: Form 4D 14
ORRELL 4H 27
Orrell Hill La. L38: Ince B 3E 17
Orrell La. L40: Burs 2D 18
Orrell M. L40: Burs 2E 19
ORRELL POST 2H 27
Orrell Rd. WN5: Orr 2H 27
Orrell Rugby Union Football Ground . . .4H 27
Orrell Station (Rail) 5H 27
Orwell Cl. L37: Form 6C 14
Osborne Rd. L37: Form 6D 14
   PR8: Ains .5B 10
Ottery Cl. PR9: Marsh 2E 5
Outlook, The L38: High 3B 16
Ovington Dr. PR8: South 6C 8
Owen Av. L39: Orm 3F 21
Oxford Ct. PR8: B'dale 5F 7
Oxford Gdns. PR8: B'dale 5E 7
Oxford Rd. PR8: B'dale 4E 7
   WN8: Skel .4C 24
Oxhouse Rd. WN5: Orr 5H 27

P

Paddock, The L37: Form 2F 15
   L39: Augh .6C 20
   PR8: Ains .1D 12
Paddock Rd. WN8: Skel 4A 26
Padstow Cl. PR9: Marsh 2E 5
Page Ct. L37: Form 4E 15
Palace Rd. PR8: B'dale 4E 7
Palais Bldgs. L40: Burs 2E 19
Palatine Rd. PR8: B'dale 4F 7
Palm Ct. WN8: Skel 3C 24
Palmerston Rd. PR9: South 3D 8
Palm Gro. PR8: South 3C 8
Paradise La. L37: Form 1E 15
Parbold Cl. L40: Burs 4F 19
Pardoe Ct. L40: Burs 4F 19
Park & Ride
   Esplanade, The 2F 7
Park Av. L37: Form 6E 15
   L39: Orm .4E 21
   PR9: South .6C 4
Park Cl. L37: Form 6D 14
Park Ct. PR9: South 1B 8
Park Cres. PR9: South 6B 4
Park Cres. Ct. PR9: South 6C 4
Parker Cres. L39: Orm 2E 21
Parkfield Cl. L39: Orm 6C 20
Parklands PR9: South 1C 8
   WN8: Skel .3H 25
Park Link L39: Augh 2D 22
Park Pool L39: Orm 4E 21
Park Rd. L37: Form 6D 14
   L39: Orm .4E 21
   PR9: South .6B 4
Park Rd. W. PR9: South 6A 4
Parkside Av. WN8: Skel 5B 24
Parkside Ct. PR9: South 6B 4
Park Wall Rd. L37: Thorn 6H 17
   L38: Ince B, Thorn 4H 17
Park Way L37: Form 6E 15
Parliament St. WN8: Uph 1G 27
Parrs La. L39: Augh 3F 23
Parsonage Brow WN8: Uph 1D 26
Parsonage Cl. WN8: Uph 2E 27
Parsonage Rd. WN8: Uph 2E 27
Part St. PR8: South 4G 7
Pasture La. L37: Form 1H 15
Pastures, The PR9: Cros 2H 5

Patterdale Cl.—Rutland Rd.

Patterdale Cl. PR8: Ains 2D **12**
Paul's La. PR9: Chu 4D **4**
Paxton Pl. WN8: Skel 5A **26**
Peacehaven WN8: Skel 4C **24**
Peak Climbing Cen. **5B 24**
Peel Rd. WN8: Skel 4B **26**
Peel St. PR8: South 3D **8**
Peet Av. L39: Orm 5D **20**
Peets La. PR9: Chu 6E **5**
Pendle Dr. L39: Orm 3G **21**
Pendle Pl. WN8: Skel 5B **26**
Penketh Pl. WN8: Skel 4A **26**
Pennine Pl. WN8: Skel 3A **26**
Pennington Av. L39: Orm 3E **21**
Pennington Ct. L39: Orm 3E **21**
(not continuous)
PENNYLANDS **4B 24**
Penrith Av. PR8: Ains 2E **13**
Penrose Pl. WN8: Skel 5C **26**
Penty Pl. PR8: South 3H **7**
Penwell Fold WN8: Skel 1C **26**
Percival Ct. PR8: South 3G **7**
Pershore Gro. PR8: Ains 1C **12**
Peters Av. L40: Burs 3E **19**
Petworth Rd. PR8: Ains 5B **10**
Philip Dr. PR8: Ains 5F **11**
Phillips Cl. L37: Form 5E **15**
Phillip's La. L37: Form 5D **14**
Phoenix Theatre **5F 25**
Pickles Dr. L40: Burs 3D **18**
Piercefield Ct. L37: Form 2E **15**
Piercefield Rd. L37: Form 3E **15**
Pikelaw Pl. WN8: Skel 4A **26**
Pilkington Rd. PR8: South 4B **8**
Pilling Cl. PR9: Marsh 2D **4**
Pilling Pl. WN8: Skel 4A **26**
Pimbo Ind. Est. WN8: Skel 4A **26**
Pimbo La. WN8: Uph 6D **26**
Pimbo Rd. WN8: Skel 4A **26**
Pine Av. L39: Orm 2F **21**
Pine Cl. WN8: Skel 4D **24**
Pine Crest L39: Augh 1D **22**
Pine Dr. L39: Orm 3F **21**
Pine Gro. L39: Orm 2F **21**
PR9: South 2B **8**
Pinewood WN8: Skel 2H **25**
Pinewood Av. L37: Form 5C **14**
Pinewood Cl. L37: Form 5C **14**
Pinfold Cl. PR8: Ains 2D **12**
Pinfold La. PR8: Ains 2C **12**
(not continuous)
Pinfold Pl. WN8: Skel 5B **26**
Pippin St. L40: Burs 5A **18**
Pit Hey Pl. WN8: Skel 4A **26**
Pitts Ho. La. PR9: Chu 1F **9**
Pitt St. PR9: South 3D **8**
Plantation Rd. L40: Burs 3B **18**
Platts La. L40: Burs 5D **18**
Platts La. Ind. Est. L40: Burs 5D **18**
Pleasureland **2F 7**
Plex La. L39: Hals 4F **13**
Plex Moss La. PR8: Ains, Hals 4F **13**
Plex Moss La. Cvn. Pk. PR8: Ains 4F **13**
Pontins Southport Cen. **6A 10**
POOL HEY **6F 9**
Pool Hey Cvn. Pk. PR9: South 5G **9**
Pool Hey La. PR8: South 6E **9**
PR9: South 6E **9**
Poolside Wlk. PR9: Cros 3G **5**
Pool St. PR9: Cros 2G **5**
Poplar Bank PR9: South 6B **4**
Poplar Dr. WN8: Skel 4D **24**
Poplars, The L40: Burs 5E **19**
Poplar St. PR8: South 4C **8**
Poppy Cl. PR8: South 1H **11**
Portland St. PR8: South 3G **7**
Post Office Av. PR9: South 2H **7**
Potter Pl. WN8: Skel 4B **26**
Poulton Ct. PR9: South 2D **8**
Poulton Rd. PR9: South 2D **8**
Preesall Cl. PR9: Marsh 3D **4**
Premier Bowl **1G 7**
Prescot Grn. L39: Orm 6D **20**
Prescot Rd. L39: Augh, Orm 1F **23**
Prescott Rd. WN8: Skel 4D **26**
Prestbury Av. PR8: Ains 6B **10**
Preston New Rd. PR9: Cros, Chu 5E **5**
Preston Rd. PR9: South 1C **8**
Prestwood Pl. WN8: Skel 5D **26**
Priesthouse Cl. L37: Form 4F **15**
Priesthouse La. L37: Form 4F **15**
Primrose Cl. L37: Form 2G **15**
PR9: Cros 1G **5**
PRIMROSE HILL **1A 20**
Prince Charles Gdns. PR8: B'dale 4F **7**
Princes Gdns. PR8: South 3C **8**
Princess Ct. PR9: South 1B **8**
Princes St. PR8: South 3G **7**
Priorswood Pl. WN8: Skel 5D **26**
Priory Cl. L37: Form 5G **15**
L40: Burs 2D **18**
Priory Ct. PR8: South 3F **7**
Priory Gdns. PR8: B'dale 5F **7**
Priory Grange PR8: B'dale 5G **7**
Priory Gro. L39: Orm 5D **20**
Priory M. PR8: South 3F **7**
Priory Nook WN8: Uph 2G **27**
Priory Rd. WN8: Uph 2G **27**
Proctor Rd. L37: Form 3B **14**
Promenade PR8: Ains 5A **10**
PR8: South 2G **7**
PR9: South 6A **4**
Prospect Pl. WN8: Skel 4D **26**
Pygon's Hill La. L31: Lyd 6A **22**

Q

Quarry Dr. L39: Augh 3E **23**
Quarry Mt. L39: Orm 3G **21**
Quays, The L40: Burs 2E **19**
Queen Anne St. PR8: South 2H **7**
Queen Charlotte Vs. PR8: Ains 6C **10**
Queens Av. L37: Form 2D **14**
Queens Ct. L39: Orm 5E **21**
QUEENSCOURT HOSPICE **5D 8**
Queens Cft. L37: Form 5C **14**
Queen's Hotel Ct. PR9: South 1H **7**
Queens Rd. L37: Form 5C **14**
PR9: South 1A **8**
WN5: Orr 4G **27**
Queen St. L39: Orm 5E **21**
Quinton Cl. PR8: Ains 1C **12**

R

Rabbit La. L40: Burs 4A **18**
Radnor Dr. PR9: Chu 4D **4**
Railway App. L39: Orm 4F **21**
Railway Path L39: Orm 6E **21**
Railway Rd. L39: Orm 4F **21**
WN8: Skel 4A **24**
Railway St. PR8: South 4G **7**
Railway Ter. PR8: South 4G **7**
Ralph's Wife's La. PR9: Banks 1H **5**
Ranelagh Dr. PR8: Ains 4F **11**
Ranslett Ct. L37: Form 4F **15**
Rathbone Rd. L38: High 3B **16**
Rathmore Cres. PR9: Chu 4F **5**
Ravenhead Dr. WN8: Uph 2E **27**
Ravenhead Way WN8: Uph 3D **26**
Raven Meols La. L37: Form 5D **14**
Ravens, The L37: Form 6E **15**
Ravenscroft L37: Form 5E **15**
Ravenscroft Av. L39: Orm 5E **21**
Rawlinson Ct. *PR9: South 1B 8*
(off Rawlinson Rd.)
Rawlinson Gro. PR9: South 6C **4**
Rawlinson Rd. PR9: South 1B **8**
Rectory Rd. PR9: Chu 6D **4**
Red Barnes L37: Form 2E **15**
Redcar Cl. PR8: South 6D **8**
Red Cat La. L40: Burs 1E **19**
Redcliffe Gdns. L39: Augh 6E **21**
Red Fold L39: Augh 6C **20**
Redgate L37: Form 5F **15**
L39: Orm 4D **20**
Redgate Dr. L37: Form 5G **15**
Redhill Dr. PR8: South 6D **8**
Red Sands L39: Augh 6D **20**
Redwood Dr. L39: Orm 5D **20**
Reeds, The L39: Orm 3D **20**
Rees Pk. L40: Burs 4F **19**
Regal Ct. PR8: Ains 6D **10**
Regency Gdns. PR8: B'dale 5E **7**
Regent Cl. PR8: B'dale 5F **7**
Regent Ct. PR9: South 1A **8**
Regent M. PR8: B'dale 5F **7**
Regent Rd. PR8: B'dale 5E **7**
Regents Fld. L37: Form 2C **14**
Renfrey Cl. L39: Orm 1E **21**
Ribble Av. PR9: Cros 3G **5**
Richmond Av. L40: Burs 4E **19**
Richmond Cl. L38: High 5B **16**
Richmond Ct. L40: Burs 4E **19**
Richmond M. L40: Burs 4F **19**
Richmond Rd. PR8: B'dale 1F **11**
Rickerby Ct. PR9: South 1A **8**
Ridge Cl. PR9: Cros 2G **5**
Ridings, The PR9: Chu 4E **5**
Riding St. PR8: South 3H **7**
Rimmer's Av. L37: Form 1D **14**
PR8: South 3H **7**
RING O'BELLS **5H 19**
Ring O'Bells La. L40: Lath 5H **19**
Ringtail Ct. L40: Burs 3B **18**
Ringtail Ind. Est. L40: Burs 5B **18**
Ringtail Pl. L40: Burs 3B **18**
Ringtail Rd. L40: Burs 3A **18**
Ripon Cl. PR8: South 6D **8**
River Cl. L37: Form 6G **15**
Rivermeade PR8: South 5B **8**
Riverside L38: High 3B **16**
Rivington Cl. PR8: B'dale 6G **7**
Rivington Dr. L40: Burs 4E **19**
WN8: Uph 2G **27**
ROBBINS BRIDGE **6A 22**
Roe La. PR9: Chu, South 1C **8**
PR9: South 1C **8**
Roe Pk. M. PR9: South 1B **8**
Romiley Dr. WN8: Skel 3D **24**
Romsey Av. L37: Form 5G **15**
Rookery Rd. PR9: South 6C **4**
Rosebay Cl. L37: Form 4F **15**
Rosebery St. PR9: South 3E **9**
Rose Cres. PR8: Ains 3E **13**
WN8: Skel 4C **24**
Rosecroft Cl. L39: Orm 3E **21**
Rose Hill PR8: South 3B **8**
Rosehill Bus. Pk. PR9: South 3B **8**
Rosehill Dr. L39: Augh 1E **23**
Roselea Dr. PR9: Cros 3G **5**
Rosemary La. L37: Form 4D **14**
Rose Path L37: Form 5F **15**
Rose Pl. L39: Augh 1F **23**
Rose Theatre **6G 21**
Rosewood PR9: Chu 5D **4**
Rostron Cres. L37: Form 6D **14**
Rothley Av. PR8: Ains 1C **12**
Rothwell Cl. L39: Orm 4D **20**
Rothwell Dr. L39: Augh 1D **22**
PR8: Ains 6A **10**
Rotten Row PR8: South 4E **7**
Rough La. L39: Bart 4F **13**
Roundway, The L38: High 4B **16**
Rowan Cl. L40: Burs 1F **19**
Rowan La. WN8: Skel 1F **25**
Rowans, The L39: Augh 4C **22**
Royal Birkdale Golf Course **2C 10**
Royal Cl. L37: Form 6F **15**
Royal Cres. L37: Form 6F **15**
Royal Pk. PR8: B'dale 5E **7**
Royal Ter. PR8: South 2G **7**
Ruddington Rd. PR8: South 6C **8**
Ruff La. L39: Orm 5F **21**
Rufford Rd. PR9: Cros 4G **5**
Russell Av. PR9: South 2E **9**
Russell Ct. PR9: Cros 3G **5**
Russell Rd. PR9: South 2E **9**
Rutland Cres. L39: Orm 2D **20**
Rutland Rd. PR8: South 4B **8**

A-Z Southport 37

Ryburn Rd. L39: Orm 6D 20
Rydal Av. L37: Form 4C 14
Ryder Cl. L39: Augh 1E 23
Ryder Cres. L39: Augh 2E 23
   PR8: B'dale 3E 11
Rydinge, The L37: Form 1F 15
Ryeground La. L37: Form 2F 15
Rymers Grn. L37: Form 3D 14

S

Sagar Fold L39: Augh 3F 23
St Andrew's Ct. PR8: South 3H 7
St Andrew's Pl. PR8: South 3H 7
St Annes Cl. L37: Form 1E 15
St Annes Path L37: Form 1E 15
St Annes Rd. L37: Form 1E 15
   L39: Orm .5D 20
   PR9: Chu 3D 4
St Bedes Cl. L39: Orm 6D 20
St Clair Dr. PR9: Chu 6E 5
St Cuthbert's Cl. PR9: Chu 5E 5
St Cuthbert's Rd. PR9: Chu 5E 5
St George's Pl. PR9: South 2H 7
St George's Rd. L37: Form 3D 14
   L38: High .2B 16
St Helens Rd. L39: Orm 4F 21
St James Cl. L40: Westh 6H 21
St James Rd. WN5: Orr 5H 27
St James St. PR8: South 3H 7
St Johns Ct. PR8: Ains 1F 13
St John's Rd. PR8: B'dale 2F 11
ST JOSEPHS HOSPICE (HETTINGA HOUSE)
   . . . . .3H 21
St Lukes Chu. Rd. L37: Form 5B 14
            (not continuous)
St Lukes Dr. L37: Form 5B 14
   WN5: Orr .5H 27
St Luke's Gro. PR8: South 2C 8
St Luke's Rd. PR9: South 3B 8
St Marys Gdns. PR8: Ains 4F 11
St Michael Rd. L39: Augh 5B 22
St Michael's Cl. PR9: Chu 4D 4
St Michaels Pk. L39: Augh 4C 22
St Pauls Mansion PR8: South 3G 7
St Paul's Pas. PR8: South 3G 7
St Paul's Sq. PR8: South 3G 7
St Paul's St. PR8: South 3G 7
St Peter's Av. L37: Form 3C 14
St Peter's Cl. L37: Form 3C 14
St Peter's Rd. PR8: B'dale 6G 7
St Stephen's St. L38: High 3B 16
St Thomas's Ct. WN8: Uph 3G 27
St Vincent's Way PR8: B'dale 5G 7
St Wyburn Ct. PR8: B'dale 3F 7
Salcombe Dr. PR9: Marsh 2E 5
Salford Ct. PR8: Ains 6C 10
Salford Rd. PR8: Ains 6C 10
Salisbury St. PR9: South 3E 9
Sallowfields WN5: Orr 4H 27
Sally's La. PR9: Chu 5E 5
Salwick Cl. PR9: Marsh 2D 4
Sambourn Fold PR8: Ains 6A 10
Sandbrook Gdns. WN5: Orr 4H 27
Sandbrook Rd. PR8: Ains 2E 13
   WN5: Orr .4G 27
Sandbrook Way PR8: Ains 2E 13
Sandfield Cotts. L39: Augh 1F 23
Sandfield Pk. L39: Augh 1F 23
Sandford Rd. WN5: Orr 4G 27
Sandheys Dr. PR9: South 6D 4
Sandhills L38: High 4B 16
Sandhurst Ct. L37: Form 6B 14
Sandilands Gro. L38: High 4B 16
Sandiway Ct. PR9: South 1C 8
Sandon Rd. PR8: B'dale 2F 11
Sandown Ct. PR9: South 1A 8
Sandringham Ct. PR9: South 1A 8
Sandringham Rd. L37: Form 6D 14
   PR8: Ains .6C 10
   PR8: B'dale .6E 7
Sandy La. L38: High 3C 16
   L39: Augh 5D 22

Sandy La. WN5: Orr 5H 27
   WN8: Skel .4B 24
Sandy La. Cen. WN8: Skel 4B 24
Sanfield Cl. L39: Orm 3E 21
Sangness Dr. PR8: South 6C 8
Sanvino Av. PR8: Ains 6D 10
Saunders St. PR9: South 6A 4
Savon Hook L37: Form 6F 15
Sawdon Av. PR8: South 5C 8
Saxenholme PR8: B'dale 4F 7
Saxon Lodge PR8: B'dale 4F 7
Saxon Rd. PR8: B'dale 4F 7
Scaffold La. L38: Ince B 1D 16
Scarisbrick Av. PR8: South 2G 7
Scarisbrick Ct. PR8: South 3A 8
Scarisbrick Ho. L39: Orm 4F 21
Scarisbrick New Rd. PR8: South 3A 8
Scarisbrick St. L39: Orm 3E 21
   PR9: South 2H 7
Scarth Hill La. L39: Augh, Westh 2G 23
   L40: Westh 6H 21
Scarth Pk. WN8: Skel 6G 25
School Av. L37: Form 4E 15
School Cl. L39: Augh 2D 22
   PR8: B'dale 1H 11
School Ho. Grn. L39: Orm 4F 21
School Ho. Gro. L40: Burs 2D 18
School La. L37: Form 4E 15
   L40: Burs .2E 19
   WN8: Skel .3B 24
   WN8: Uph .2G 27
School Rd. L38: High 3B 16
Scott St. PR9: South 2E 9
Scott Dr. L39: Orm 2F 21
Seabank Rd. PR9: South 1H 7
Seacroft Cres. PR9: Marsh 2F 5
Seafield L37: Form 5F 15
Seafield Rd. PR8: Ains 5C 10
Sealand Av. L37: Form 5C 14
Sealand Cl. L37: Form 5C 14
Seaton Pl. WN8: Skel 2C 24
Seaton Way PR9: Marsh 2E 5
Seddon Pl. WN8: Skel 2C 24
Sefton Av. WN5: Orr 4H 27
Sefton Cl. WN5: Orr 4H 27
Sefton Gdns. L39: Augh 4F 23
Sefton Ho. L40: Burs 2E 19
Sefton Rd. L37: Form 5D 14
   WN5: Orr .4H 27
Sefton St. PR8: South 5H 7
Sefton Vw. WN5: Orr 4H 27
Segar's La. PR8: Ains 6D 10
Selby Dr. L37: Form 5G 15
Selby Pl. WN8: Skel 2B 24
Selworthy Rd. PR8: B'dale 6D 6
Sephton Dr. L39: Orm 2F 21
            (not continuous)
Serpentine, The L39: Augh 3F 23
Sevenoaks Av. PR8: Ains 6B 10
Shaftesbury Av. PR8: B'dale 3G 11
Shaftesbury Gro. PR8: B'dale 2G 11
Shaftesbury Rd. PR8: B'dale 3G 11
Shakespeare Cen., The PR8: South 4H 7
Shakespeare St. PR8: South 4H 7
Sharrock St. PR8: South 2H 7
Shaw Cres. L37: Form 3G 15
Shaw's Av. PR8: B'dale 2G 11
Shaw's Rd. PR8: B'dale 2G 11
Shelley Dr. L39: Orm 3D 20
Shelley Gro. PR8: South 2D 8
Shellfield Rd. PR9: Chu 4E 5
Shelton Dr. PR8: Ains 1C 12
Shenley Way PR9: Cros 2H 5
Sherborne Rd. WN8: Skel 4B 24
Sherringham Rd. PR8: B'dale 1E 11
Sherwood Av. L39: Augh 1E 23
Sherwood Dr. WN8: Skel 5B 24
Sherwood Ho. PR8: Ains 6C 10
Sherwood Lodge PR8: B'dale 4F 7
Shirdley Cres. PR8: Ains 2E 13
Shireburn Rd. L37: Form 2B 14
Shirewell Rd. WN5: Orr 4H 27
Shore Rd. PR8: Ains 5A 10
Sidney Rd. PR9: South 1D 8

Silcock's Funland 1G 7
Silverdale PR8: B'dale 5E 7
Silverdale Ct. PR8: South 5C 8
Silverthorne Dr. PR9: South 6D 4
Simpson's Pl. PR8: South 3H 7
Sixpenny La. L39: Bart 4F 13
Sixteen Acre La. L37: Form 1F 15
SKELMERSDALE 4F 25
Skelmersdale Hall Dr. WN8: Skel 2D 24
Skelmersdale Hall Rd. WN8: Skel 2E 25
Skelmersdale Rd. WN8: Skel 6A 24
Skelmersdale Sports Cen. 6G 25
Skipton Av. PR9: Cros 1G 5
Slackey's La. PR9: Cros 3G 5
Slaidburn Cres. PR9: Marsh 2E 5
Slaidburn Ind. Est. PR9: Marsh 2E 5
Slate La. WN8: Skel 2A 24
Small La. L39: Augh 6A 20
   L39: Orm .5F 21
Smethurst Hall Pk. WN5: Bil 6G 27
Smethurst Rd. WN5: Bil 6G 27
Smith St. WN8: Skel 4B 24
Smithy Cl. L37: Form 3G 15
Smithy Glen Dr. WN5: Bil 5H 27
Smithy Grn. L37: Form 3G 15
Smithy La. L39: Augh 5B 22
Smithy Wlk. L40: Burs 2E 19
Somerset Dr. PR8: Ains 3E 13
Southbank Rd. PR8: South 3H 7
Southern Rd. PR8: South 3G 7
South Hill PR8: South 3G 7
SOUTHPORT .2H 7
Southport and Ainsdale Golf Course . . .4D 10
SOUTHPORT AND FORMBY DISTRICT
   GENERAL HOSPITAL 5C 8
Southport Arts Cen. 2H 7
Southport Bus. Cen. PR9: South 2H 7
           (off Lord St.)
Southport Bus. Pk. PR8: South 6B 8
Southport Enterprise Cen. PR9: South . . .3E 9
Southport FC .4C 8
SOUTHPORT GENERAL INFIRMARY 4B 8
Southport Old Rd. L37: Form 5D 12
Southport Pier 1F 7
Southport Rd. L37: Form 2F 15
   L39: Orm .3E 21
   L40: Scar .1C 20
   PR8: Scar 6E 9
Southport Station (Rail) 2H 7
Southport Theatre & Floral Hall 1G 7
South Ter. L39: Form 5E 21
Southway WN8: Skel 4F 25
Spa La. L40: Lath 1A 24
Spencers La. WN5: Orr 2H 27
   WN8: Skel .5F 25
Sphynx Lawn Tennis Club 5C 8
Spinney, The L37: Form 2F 15
Spinney Cl. L39: Orm 6D 20
Spring Cl. PR8: B'dale 4G 7
Springfield Cl. L37: Form 5B 14
   L40: Burs .5D 18
Springfield Rd. L39: Augh 6B 22
Spruce Way L37: Form 4B 14
Spymers Cft. L37: Form 1F 15
Square La. L40: Burs 4E 19
Squirrel Grn. L37: Form 2B 14
Stafford Rd. PR8: B'dale 2G 11
Stafford St. WN8: Skel 3B 24
Stamford Rd. PR8: B'dale 6H 7
   WN8: Skel .3B 24
Standhouse La. L39: Augh 1E 23
Standside Pk. WN8: Skel 5B 24
Stanlawe Rd. L37: Form 1D 14
STANLEY 2C 24
Stanley Av. PR8: B'dale 6F 7
Stanley Ct. L40: Burs 2E 19
Stanley Ind. Est. WN8: Skel 2C 24
Stanley Rd. L37: Form 1D 14
   WN8: Uph .2F 27
Stanley St. L39: Orm 4F 21
   PR9: South 2H 7
Stanley Way WN8: Skel 2C 24
Stannanought Rd. WN8: Skel . . .2G 25 & 1C 26
            (not continuous)

Stapleton Rd. L37: Form 6B 14
Statham Rd. WN8: Skel 1B 24
Statham Way L39: Orm 5E 21
Station App. L39: Orm 4F 21
   L40: Burs 2E 19
   (not continuous)
Station Av. WN5: Orr 4H 27
Station Rd. L39: Orm 3F 21
   PR8: Ains 6C 10
Staveley Av. L40: Burs 3E 19
Staveley Rd. PR8: Ains 1F 13
   WN8: Skel 2C 24
Stephenson Way L37: Form 4G 15
Stiles, The L39: Orm 4E 21
Stirling Ct. PR9: Chu 5E 5
Stoneleigh Cl. PR8: Ains 1E 13
Stourton Rd. PR8: Ains 1E 13
Stratford Cl. PR8: Ains 5A 10
Stretton Dr. PR9: South 1D 8
Stub La. L40: Burs 5A 18
Studley Ct. PR9: South 6B 4
Sturgess Cl. L39: Orm 2F 21
Sudell La. L31: Lyd 5A 22
   L39: Augh 5A 22
Suffolk Rd. PR8: B'dale 3G 11
Sulby Cl. PR8: B'dale 6F 7
Summer St. WN8: Skel 1D 24
Sumner Rd. L37: Form 4E 15
Sunbury Dr. PR8: Ains 1D 12
Suncourt PR8: South 3F 7
Sunningdale Gdns. L37: Form 4D 14
Sunnyfields L39: Orm 4G 21
Sunny Rd. PR9: Chu 5E 5
Sunnyside L39: Augh 4E 23
   PR8: B'dale 6F 7
Sunnyside Ct. PR9: South 6A 4
Surrey Cl. PR9: Cros 2G 5
Sussex Rd. PR8: South 3B 8
   PR9: South 2A 8
Sutch La. L40: Lath 3H 19
Sutton Rd. L37: Form 6D 14
Swan All. L39: Orm 4E 21
   (off Burscough St.)
Swan Delph L39: Augh 1E 23
Swan La. L39: Augh 5A 22
Swanpool La. L39: Augh 2E 23
Swifts Fold WN8: Skel 5B 24
Sycamore Dr. WN8: Skel 3C 24
Sycamore Gro. L37: Form 6B 14

T

Tadlow Cl. L37: Form 6B 14
Talaton Cl. PR9: Marsh 2E 5
Talbot Dr. PR8: South 3H 7
Talbot St. PR8: South 4G 7
Tamneys, The WN8: Skel 4D 24
Tancaster WN8: Skel 4C 24
Tanfields WN8: Skel 4D 24
TANHOUSE 4H 25
Tanhouse Rd. WN8: Skel 5G 25
Tarleton Rd. PR9: South 1E 9
Tarlswood WN8: Skel 4D 24
Tarn Brow L39: Orm 6C 20
Tarn Rd. L37: Form 4C 14
Tarnside Rd. WN5: Orr 3H 27
Tarvin Cl. PR9: Cros 2H 5
Tavistock Dr. PR8: Ains 5B 10
TAWD BRIDGE 6G 25
Tawd Rd. WN8: Skel 5G 25
TAWD VALLEY PARK 3D 24
Taylor Av. L39: Orm 4G 21
Taylor St. WN8: Skel 4A 24
Teal Cl. L39: Augh 1E 23
Tedder Av. PR9: South 2E 9
Tellethome Ind. Est.
   L40: Burs 4B 18
Templemartin WN8: Skel 3D 24
Tenby WN8: Skel 3C 24
Tennyson Dr. L39: Orm 3D 20
Teversham WN8: Skel 3D 24
Teviot WN8: Skel 3C 24
Tewkesbury WN8: Skel 3C 24

Thanet WN8: Skel 3D 24
Thealby Cl. WN8: Skel 3C 24
Thirlmere Av. L37: Form 5F 15
   WN8: Uph 2F 27
Thirlmere Dr. PR8: Ains 2D 12
Thirlmere Rd. L38: High 3C 16
Thirsk WN8: Skel 3D 24
Thistle Ct. L40: Burs 1E 19
Thistleton M. PR9: South 1A 8
Thompson Av. L39: Orm 4G 21
Thornbeck Av. L38: High 5B 16
Thornbridge Av. L40: Burs 4E 19
Thornbury WN8: Skel 3D 24
Thornby WN8: Skel 3D 24
Thorndale WN8: Skel 3D 24
Thornhill L39: Augh 2D 22
Thornhill Cl. L39: Augh 3D 22
Thornton WN8: Skel 3D 24
Thornwood WN8: Skel 3D 24
Thoroughgood Cl. L40: Burs 5D 18
Thorpe WN8: Skel 3D 24
Three Oaks Cl. L40: Lath 5H 19
Three Pools PR9: Cros 4G 5
   (not continuous)
Three Tuns La. L37: Form 4E 15
Threlfalls La. PR9: Chu 5D 4
Thurcroft Dr. WN8: Skel 3C 24
Thursby Cl. PR8: Ains 2D 12
Thurston WN8: Skel 3C 24
Tilcroft WN8: Skel 3C 24
Timms Cl. L37: Form 2E 15
Timms La. L37: Form 2E 15
Tinsley Av. PR8: South 6C 8
Tintagel WN8: Skel 3B 24
Tintern Dr. L37: Form 5G 15
Tithebarn Rd. PR8: South 3B 8
Tithebarn St. WN8: Uph 2F 27
Tiverton Av. WN8: Skel 3C 24
Tollgate Rd. L40: Burs 5B 18
Tongbarn WN8: Skel 3C 24
TONTINE 4H 27
Tontine WN5: Orr 4G 27
Tontine Rd. WN8: Uph 3G 27
Top Acre Rd. WN8: Skel 6G 25
Torcross Cl. PR9: Marsh 2E 5
Totnes Dr. PR9: Marsh 2E 5
Tourist Info. Cen.
   Southport 2H 7
Tower Bldgs. PR9: South 1A 8
Tower End L37: Form 2B 14
Tower Hill L39: Orm 4G 21
Tower Hill Rd. WN8: Uph 4D 26
Tower Nook WN8: Uph 4E 27
Town End Cl. L39: Orm 5D 20
TOWN GREEN 4E 23
Town Grn. Ct. L39: Augh 3E 23
Town Grn. Gdns. L39: Augh 3E 23
Town Grn. La. L39: Augh 3E 23
Town Green Station (Rail) 4E 23
Town La. PR8: South 5B 8
Town La. (Kew) PR8: South 6B 8
Tracks La. WN5: Bil 6H 27
Trafalgar Ct. PR8: B'dale 6F 7
Trafalgar Rd. PR8: B'dale 1E 11
Trap Hill L37: Form 5B 14
Treen Cl. PR9: Marsh 1F 5
Treesdale Cl. PR8: B'dale 5F 7
Treetop Vs. PR9: Chu 3D 4
Trent Cl. L40: Burs 2F 19
Trevor Rd. L40: Burs 3D 18
   PR8: Ains 1E 13
Trinity Gdns. PR8: South 3G 7
Trinity M. PR9: South 2A 8
Truro Av. PR9: Marsh 2F 5
Truscott Rd. L40: Burs 3D 18
Tudor Gdns. L38: High 3B 16
Tudor Mans. PR8: South 3F 7
Tudor Rd. PR8: Ains 5B 10
Tulketh St. PR8: South 2H 7
Turnacre L37: Form 1G 15
Turnberry WN8: Skel 3B 24
Turnberry Way PR9: Cros 2H 5
Turnpike Rd. L39: Augh 2C 22

Twistfield Cl. PR8: B'dale 4F 7
Two Saints Pl. L39: Orm 4E 21
Tyrer Rd. L39: Orm 2F 21
Tyrers Cl. L37: Form 5E 15

U

Uldale Cl. PR8: Ains 2D 12
Union St. PR9: South 1A 8
Unit Rd. PR8: Ains 6D 10
UP HOLLAND 2G 27
Upholland Rd. WN5: Bil 5H 27
Upholland Station (Rail) 5D 26
Up. Aughton Rd. PR8: B'dale 4G 7
Uppingham WN8: Skel 4B 24
Upton Av. PR8: Ains 5B 10

V

Vale Cres. PR8: Ains 3E 13
Vale La. L40: Lath 1B 24
   (not continuous)
Varlian Cl. L40: Westh 6H 21
Vaughan Cl. L37: Form 3C 14
Vaughan Rd. PR8: B'dale 5H 7
Vernon Ct. PR8: South 4B 8
Vernon Rd. PR9: South 1E 9
Verulam Rd. PR9: Chu 4F 5
Vicarage Cl. L37: Form 3C 14
   L40: Westh 6H 21
Vicarage Gdns. L40: Burs 2D 18
   WN5: Orr 5H 27
   (off Sandy La.)
Vicarage La. L40: Westh 6H 21
Vicarage Rd. L37: Form 3C 14
   WN5: Orr 5H 27
Vicarage Wlk. L39: Orm 4E 21
Viceroy Ct. PR8: South 3G 7
Vickers Dr. WN8: Skel 1C 26
Victoria Bri. Rd. PR8: South 3A 8
Victoria Bldgs. L37: Form 2D 14
Victoria Ct. PR8: B'dale 5F 7
   (not continuous)
   WN8: Skel 4A 24
Victoria Leisure & Fitness
   Formby .4E 15
   Southport 1H 7
Victoria M. PR9: South 2B 8
Victoria Pk. 2E 19
Victoria Pk. WN8: Skel 4A 24
Victoria Rd. L37: Form 2A 14
   L38: Ince B 4G 17
   L39: Augh 6C 20
Victoria St. L40: Burs 2E 19
   PR9: South 1H 7
Victoria Way L37: Form 2C 14
   PR8: South 2F 7
Victory Av. PR9: South 2E 9
Viking Cl. PR8: B'dale 5G 7
Village Cl. WN8: Skel 5B 24
Village Row PR8: Ains 6C 10
Village Way L38: High 3B 16
   WN8: Skel 5B 24
Virginia St. PR8: South 3A 8
Vivian Dr. PR8: B'dale 1G 11
Vue Cinema
   Southport 1G 7
Vulcan Ct. PR9: South 2A 8
Vulcan St. PR9: South 2A 8

W

Waldron WN8: Skel 5B 24
Walk, The PR8: B'dale 5G 7
Walker Cl. L37: Form 5E 15
Wallcroft St. WN8: Skel 5C 24
Walmer Ct. PR8: B'dale 5F 7
Walmer Rd. PR8: B'dale 6G 7
Walnut St. PR8: South 5A 8
Walro M. PR9: Chu 4E 5
Walton St. PR9: South 1A 8

Ward Av. L37: Form 5C **14**
Warper's Moss Cl. L40: Burs 2F **19**
Warper's Moss La. L40: Burs 2F **19**
Warren Ct. PR8: B'dale 4E **7**
Warren Grn. L37: Form 3C **14**
Warren Rd. PR9: South 1E **9**
Warwick Cl. PR8: South 5H **7**
Warwick St. PR8: South 5H **7**
Washbrook Way L39: Orm 5E **21**
Watchyard La. L37: Form 4F **15**
Waterfoot Av. PR8: Ains 2D **12**
Water La. PR9: Cros 2H **5**
Waterloo Rd. PR8: B'dale 1E **11**
Watermede WN5: Bil 6H **27**
Waterworks Rd. L39: Orm 3G **21**
Wavell Av. PR9: South 2F **9**
Wavell Cl. PR9: South 2F **9**
Waverley WN8: Skel 4B **24**
Waverley St. PR8: South 2G **7**
Wayfarers Arc. PR8: South 2H **7**
Weaver Av. L40: Burs 2F **19**
Welbeck Rd. PR8: B'dale 5F **7**
Welbeck Ter. PR8: South 5G **7**
Welbourne WN8: Skel 5B **24**
Weldale Ho. *PR8: B'dale* *5F* ***7***
 (off Chase Cl.)
Weld Dr. L37: Form 3C **14**
Weldon Dr. L39: Orm 5F **21**
Weld Pde. PR8: B'dale 5F **7**
Weld Rd. PR8: B'dale 4E **7**
Wellcross Rd. WN8: Uph 3F **27**
Wellfield La. L40: Westh 6H **21**
Wellington Cl. WN8: Skel 1C **26**
Wellington St. PR8: South 3G **7**
Welwyn Av. PR8: Ains 5E **11**
Wennington Rd. PR9: South 1D **8**
Wentworth Cl. PR8: Ains 1E **13**
Wescoe Cl. WN5: Orr 4H **27**
Wesley St. PR8: South 2H **7**
Westbourne Gdns. PR8: B'dale 5D **6**
Westbourne Rd. PR8: B'dale 5D **6**
Westcliffe Ct. PR8: South 4F **7**
Westcliffe Rd. PR8: B'dale 4E **7**
Westdene PR9: South 6B **4**
West End Ter. PR8: South 2G **7**
Westgate WN8: Skel 4B **24**
Westgate Dr. WN5: Orr 4H **27**
Westgate Ind. Est. WN8: Skel 5B **24**
WEST GILLIBRANDS 5B **24**
Westhaven Cres. L39: Augh 2E **23**
West Hill PR8: South 3G **7**
Westholme Ct. PR9: South 6A **4**
West Lancashire Yacht Club 1G **7**
Westminster Dr. PR8: Ains 6A **10**
Westmoreland Rd. PR8: South 4A **8**
West Pk. PR9: South 6B **4**
West Pk. Cl. WN8: Skel 5B **24**
WEST PIMBO 5B **26**
Westridge Ct. PR9: South 1B **8**
West St. PR8: South 2G **7**
West Vw. L39: Orm 4F **21**
West Way L38: High 3B **16**
Westwood Cl. PR8: South 6C **8**

Whalley Dr. L37: Form 5F **15**
 L39: Augh 3E **23**
WHALLEYS 1F **25**
Whalleys Rd. WN8: Skel 1F **25**
Wheatacre WN8: Skel 5C **24**
Wheat La. L40: Lath 4G **19**
Wheatsheaf Wlk. *L39: Orm* *4E* ***21***
Whelmar Ho. WN8: Skel 4G **25**
Whitburn WN8: Skel 4B **24**
Whitby Av. PR9: Cros 1G **5**
Whitefield Cl. L38: High 5B **16**
Whitehaven Cl. PR8: Ains 2D **12**
Whitehey WN8: Skel 5C **24**
Whitehey Rd. WN8: Skel 5C **24**
Whitehouse Av. L37: Form 4F **15**
Whitehouse La. L37: Form 4F **15**
Whiteledge Rd. WN8: Skel 6F **25**
WHITE MOSS 6C **24**
Whitemoss Bus. Pk. WN8: Skel 6C **24**
White Moss Rd. WN8: Skel 5A **24**
White Moss Rd. Sth. WN8: Skel 6A **24**
Whiterails Dr. L39: Orm 3D **20**
Whiterails M. L39: Orm 3D **20**
Whitestocks WN8: Skel 5C **24**
Whitstone Dr. WN8: Skel 6H **25**
Whittle Dr. L37: Orm 2E **21**
Wicks Cres. L37: Form 3B **14**
Wicks Gdns. L37: Form 4D **14**
Wicks Grn. L37: Form 4B **14**
Wicks Grn. Cl. L37: Form 3B **14**
Wicks La. L37: Form 4A **14**
 (not continuous)
Wigan Rd. L39: Orm 4F **21**
 WN8: Skel 5D **24**
Wight Moss Way PR8: South 6B **8**
Wignalls Mdw. L38: High 4B **16**
Wigston Cl. PR8: Ains 1D **12**
Wilcove WN8: Skel 4D **24**
Willard Av. WN5: Bil 6H **27**
Willow Cres. L40: Burs 1F **19**
Willow Dr. WN8: Skel 4C **24**
Willow End L40: Burs 3F **19**
Willow Grn. L39: Orm 4F **21**
 PR9: Cros 3G **5**
Willow Gro. L37: Form 3E **15**
 PR8: South 2C **8**
Willow Hey WN8: Skel 4D **24**
Willowhey PR9: Chu 3D **4**
Willows, The *PR8: South* *3F* ***7***
 (off Beechfield Gdns.)
Willow Wlk. WN8: Skel 1F **25**
Wilmcote Gro. PR8: Ains 1D **12**
Wilsham Rd. WN5: Orr 4H **27**
Wimbrick Cl. L39: Orm 5D **20**
Wimbrick Cres. L39: Orm 6D **20**
Windermere Cres. PR8: Ains 2E **13**
Windermere Rd. L38: High 3C **16**
Windgate WN8: Skel 5D **24**
Windmill Av. L39: Orm 4F **21**
Windmill Hgts. WN8: Uph 1E **27**
Windmill Ho. PR9: Chu 4D **4**
Windmill Rd. WN8: Uph 2D **26**
Windrows WN8: Skel 4D **24**
Windsor Cl. L40: Burs 4E **19**

Windsor Ct. PR8: B'dale 5E **7**
Windsor Rd. L37: Form 5D **14**
 PR9: South 3B **8**
 WN8: Uph 1E **27**
Windy Harbour Rd. PR8: B'dale 4E **11**
Winifred La. L39: Augh 2C **22**
Winstanley Rd. WN5: Bil 5H **27**
Winsters, The WN8: Skel 4D **24**
Winston Cres. PR8: South 6C **8**
Witham Rd. WN8: Skel 4A **24**
Withins Fld. L38: High 4B **16**
Withins La. L38: Gt Alt 1H **17**
Wollaton Dr. PR8: South 6D **8**
Wolverton WN8: Skel 5D **24**
Woodcroft WN8: Skel 5D **24**
Woodfield Rd. L39: Orm 6D **20**
Woodhouses L38: High 4B **16**
Woodland Path L37: Ains, Form ...4B **12**
Woodlands, The L40: Burs 4G **19**
 PR8: Ains 6C **10**
Woodlands Cl. L37: Form 4C **14**
 L39: Orm 5G **21**
 PR9: South 1B **8**
Woodlands Rd. L37: Form 5C **14**
Woodlea Cl. PR9: Cros 2H **5**
Woodley Pk. Rd. WN8: Skel 1F **25**
Wood Moss La. L40: Scar 6H **9**
Woodrow WN8: Skel 5C **24**
Woodside Av. PR8: Ains 2D **12**
Woodside Cl. WN8: Uph 1G **27**
Woodstock Dr. PR8: B'dale 3F **11**
WOODVALE 2E **13**
Woodvale Rd. PR8: Ains 3E **13**
Woodvale Sidings PR8: Ains ...4F **13**
Wordsworth Cl. L39: Orm 3D **20**
Worthing Cl. PR8: B'dale 6F **7**
Wrights Ter. PR8: B'dale 6H **7**
Wright St. PR9: South 2H **7**
Wrigleys Cl. L37: Form 2E **15**
Wrigleys La. L37: Form 2E **15**
Wyke Cop Rd. PR8: South 5H **9**
 PR9: South 5H **9**
Wyke La. PR9: South ..1G **9** & 5H **9**
Wyresdale Av. PR8: South 5B **8**

Y

Yellow Ho. La. PR8: South 3H **7**
Yewdale WN8: Skel 4E **25**
Yew Tree Rd. L39: Orm 2E **21**
York Av. PR8: South 4G **7**
York Cl. L37: Form 1E **15**
York Gdns. PR8: B'dale 4G **7**
York Mnr. L37: Form 4E **15**
 PR8: B'dale 4G **7**
York Rd. L37: Form 4E **15**
 PR8: B'dale 5F **7**
York Ter. PR9: South 1A **8**

Z

Zetland St. PR9: South 2B **8**